MACHU PICCHU
TRAVEL GUIDE 2023

An Ultimate Insider's Handbook to discover
the Hidden Wonders, Enchanting Landscapes,
Cultural Heritage, and Insider Tips for
Adventurers

ANDREA TOWNSON

TABLE OF CONTENTS

CHAPTER TEN

CONCLUSION

MEMORIES FOR A LIFETIME

INTRODUCTION

A destination like no other inspires the imagination like the beautiful Andes, where the whispers of ancient civilizations resonate through time. It is a place of wonder and mystery, where history's walls reveal their secrets to those who dare to enter. It is the mythical Machu Picchu, an ethereal site that leaves an everlasting impact on the souls of those who are fortunate enough to walk its holy grounds.

Imagine a tourist, driven by an insatiable wanderlust, setting foot on this holy ground. They are breathless as the first rays of the sun pour their golden glow across the ancient stronghold, unable to comprehend the absolute majesty that surrounds them. The air crackles with excitement, and a sense of respect pervades every movement.

Our daring explorer ascends the stone steps, each one a tribute to the Inca civilization's resourcefulness. They are stunned by the sheer scope of human effort as they trace the curves of the terraces, a sophisticated network of agricultural prowess. How did these prehistoric people create such complex routes through the harsh mountainside? The intellect is full with questions, and the heart longs for answers.

As the pilgrim progresses deeper into the mythical region of Machu Picchu, he or she sees cryptic buildings that transcend conventional comprehension. The golden-hued Temple of the Sun appears to carry the wisdom of the centuries inside its walls. The Intihuatana, a stone sundial, whispers secrets to those who listen carefully, implying an intimate relationship with the celestial powers that govern our world. The ruins of a long-lost civilization beckon them at every step, beckoning them to discover the mysteries of the past.

But Machu Picchu is more than simply a time capsule. As the surrounding peaks stand tall, shrouded in emerald-green vegetation, it is a living tribute to nature's tenacity. As birds flit over the lush flora, serenading the explorers with their enchanting songs, the traveler finds consolation in the symphony of sounds. One cannot but experience a profound sense of oneness in the presence of this stunning natural backdrop, an understanding of the fragile balance that maintains life on this world.

The traveler sits atop one of the ancient terraces, watching the great expanse below, as the day fades to twilight. The sunset sun's warm hues paint the sky, creating a spell of enchantment over the ruins. They soak in the heady air, filled with the echoes of the past, and ponder on their incredible voyage.

Machu Picchu, a monument to human ingenuity and natural grandeur, has left an unforgettable imprint on our daring explorer. The trip has been one of self-discovery and inquiry, a pilgrimage to a place where time stops still and the distinctions between the present and the past fade into insignificance. It is a site that reminds us of the human spirit's infinite potential and the lasting impact we leave behind.

Allow the echoes of Machu Picchu to remain in your heart, dear wanderer. Allow them to inspire you to seek out the world's hidden beauties, to immerse yourself in the rich tapestry of cultures and landscapes waiting to be discovered. And, when you go on your own journey, keep in mind that the actual essence of travel rests not only in the places we see, but also in the transformational influence they have upon us.

Welcome to Machu Picchu

Welcome to Machu Picchu, a mesmerizing realm where history and mysticism merge, leaving tourists spellbound and wanting more. This ancient castle, nestled above the magnificent peaks of Peru's Andes, contains the keys to a forgotten civilization, patiently awaiting intrepid explorers to unravel its secrets.

Imagine entering a world where time seems to stand still, where the echoes of an incredible civilization echo through every stone. Machu Picchu, often known as the "Lost City of the Incas," is a tribute to a bygone era's creativity and artistry. Its elaborate stone terraces, awe-inspiring temples, and enigmatic buildings defy explanation, testing our limits of what is conceivable.

As you travel through the meandering pathways, you will be taken back in time, as if through a doorway to another dimension. The sheer magnificence of the citadel takes your breath away, leaving you in awe of the ancient Inca architects and builders' astounding feat. How did they precisely shape and fit these massive stones together? For decades, it has captivated brains, attracting archaeologists, historians, and curious people like you.

But Machu Picchu is more than just a feat of human ingenuity; it also has mystical significance. The aura that exudes from these ancient ruins is apparent, instilling awe in every stride. Standing on a terraced cliff, viewing the spreading valleys below, you can almost hear the echoes of long-forgotten ceremonies and sense the spiritual connection between the heavens and the ground.

Aside from its historical significance, Machu Picchu has a stunning natural environment. It's as if Mother

Nature herself collaborated to create a beauty, surrounded by beautiful mountains shrouded in verdant vegetation. The brilliant colors, the symphony of sounds, and the crisp mountain air all work together to create an immersive experience that awakens your senses and leaves you feeling alive.

But beware, my traveler, for the enchantment of Machu Picchu comes at a cost. The travel to this legendary haven is an adventure in and of itself. Whether you climb the famed Inca Trail, through rocky mountain passes and old stone steps, or take the panoramic train trip through the awe-inspiring Sacred Valley, each step brings you closer to a world unlike any other.

So, dare to be swept away by Machu Picchu's attraction. As you walk over its holy grounds, let its wonders unfold before your eyes. Allow yourself to be seduced by its ethereal beauty and intrigued by its ancient stories. For within these ancient ruins is a strong connection to the past, an everlasting reminder of our forefathers' tremendous achievements. Begin this remarkable adventure and allow Machu Picchu to leave an unforgettable imprint on your soul.

CHAPTER ONE

History and Importance

Machu Picchu's past is cloaked in mystery and intrigue, adding to its attractiveness and attracting the imagination of those who strive to understand its secrets. This ancient stronghold, perched high in the Andes Mountains, was erected around the 15th century by the Inca civilisation and remained hidden from the outside world for centuries.

The Inca emperor Pachacuti, a visionary leader who desired to create a refuge that would revere both the natural and spiritual realms, is thought to have inspired the construction of Machu Picchu. The complex was built with exquisite precision and intentionally placed to blend in with the surrounding terrain, incorporating the sacred peaks of Huayna Picchu and Machu Picchu into its architecture.

The rise and fall of the Inca Empire, however, resulted in the abandonment of Machu Picchu, leaving it untouched and hidden from Spanish conquistadors and succeeding colonial forces. It wasn't until 1911 that an American explorer called Hiram Bingham discovered the ruins, igniting worldwide interest in this conundrum.

Machu Picchu has become an iconic symbol of Inca civilization and a UNESCO World Heritage Site since its rediscovery. Its architectural brilliance, exquisite stonework, and elaborate terraces demonstrate the Incas' sophisticated engineering and astrological expertise. The sheer size of the complex, with over 150 structures comprising residential sections, temples, and agricultural terraces, reflects the once-thriving people that inhabited these hallowed grounds.

Machu Picchu is spiritually significant in addition to its architectural splendor. Scholars believe it was a ceremonial and pilgrimage place dedicated to the worship of Inca deities and natural veneration. The perfect alignment of its constructions with celestial events like the solstices and equinoxes reveals a sophisticated awareness of astronomical principles and a belief in the cosmos' interconnection.

Machu Picchu's ethereal beauty and profound historical significance have drawn visitors from all over the world. Every year, countless travelers undertake the perilous journey to witness the allure of this ancient wonder for themselves. Standing among the ruins, surrounded by mist-shrouded peaks, one can't help but feel wonder and veneration for the civilization that once flourished in this isolated corner of the world.

To safeguard the integrity of Machu Picchu, preservation efforts have been undertaken, including visitation limits and sustainable tourism practices. The site serves as a reminder of our common cultural heritage's importance, as well as the necessity to balance the preservation of history with the urge to discover and appreciate its beauty.

Finally, Machu Picchu is a tribute to the Inca civilization's brilliance, spirituality, and cultural richness. Its significance and history are intertwined into the fabric of human existence, enthralling hearts and minds with its immortal heritage. Machu Picchu urges us to connect with the past, embrace the marvels of human achievement, and enjoy the delicate beauty of our world's historical monuments as we continue to uncover its secrets.

Why Go to Machu Picchu?

Machu Picchu draws visitors from all over the world, providing an experience that goes beyond conventional tourism. This magnificent site has a plethora of reasons why it should be on the bucket list of every adventurer. Here are just a few strong reasons to go to Machu Picchu:

1. Timeless Wonder: Machu Picchu is a tribute to the Inca civilization's inventiveness and architectural skill. The beautiful masonry, seamless interaction with the surrounding terrain, and sheer magnitude of the complex will take your breath away. It's an opportunity to see firsthand one of the world's most spectacular archaeological sites.

2. Historical Importance: Entering Machu Picchu is like traveling back in time. This citadel maintains the legacy of a once-great empire, providing insight into the Inca people's lives and beliefs. The historical significance of the place is a fascinating glimpse into the past, arousing curiosity and wonder about the mysteries that still surround it.

3. Spiritual Connection: There is an obvious spiritual aura emanating from Machu Picchu. You can't help but sense a strong connection to something higher than yourself as you travel around its ancient temples, terraces, and sacred areas. The reverence for nature, alignment with cosmic happenings, and spiritual rites done here make it a spiritually significant location.

4. Machu Picchu is a natural wonder in and of itself, set amidst the magnificent Andean mountain range. The ancient ruins are set against a stunning landscape of lush green peaks, flowing rivers, and mist-shrouded valleys. Hiking the neighboring trails and seeing panoramic vistas will leave you

mesmerized by the natural world's overwhelming magnificence.

5. Adventure & Difficulty: The travel to Machu Picchu is an adventure in and of itself. Whether you choose to trek the renowned Inca Trail, passing by ancient ruins along the way, or take a different route, the physical and mental challenge adds to the overall sense of accomplishment and rewards you with breathtaking views and unforgettable experiences.

6. Cultural Immersion: Visiting Machu Picchu allows you to immerse yourself in Peru's rich cultural tapestry. You'll acquire a deeper understanding of the region's background and lively present-day culture by exploring the vibrant city of Cusco, originally the capital of the Inca Empire, as well as mingling with local residents and enjoying their traditions and cuisine.

7. Sunrises that stir the soul: Witnessing the sunrise at Machu Picchu is a life-changing event. You'll feel a sense of surprise and thankfulness for being a part of such a magical moment as the first rays of

sunshine wash the citadel, illuminating its ancient stones and casting a golden glow. It's an ethereal spectacle that will stay with you for the rest of your life.

Visiting Machu Picchu is a once-in-a-lifetime experience that blends history, spirituality, natural beauty, and adventure. It provides an opportunity to connect with history, marvel at human achievement, and immerse you in the wonders of a place steeped in rich traditions. Prepare to be intrigued, inspired, and forever altered by Machu Picchu's everlasting allure.

Making Travel Plans

A trip to Machu Picchu involves meticulous planning to ensure a pleasant and unforgettable experience. Here's a travel guide to help you plan your vacation to this lovely location:

1. Choose the Best Time to Visit: Machu Picchu may be visited all year, but the best time to visit depends on your preferences. The dry season, which runs

from May to September, provides sunny days and beautiful sky, but it is also the busiest. From October through April, the wet season delivers lush scenery and fewer tourists, but rain showers are more common. Consider your priorities and choose the best moment for you.

2. Determine your trip Duration: The amount of time you have available will determine the type of experience you can have at Machu Picchu. Plan to stay for at least two to three days to allow for acclimatization, exploration of other surrounding attractions, and numerous visits to the citadel itself.

3. Choose your way: The Inca Trail, a multi-day hike that requires permits and early planning, is the most famous and traditional way to Machu Picchu. Other trekking routes, such as the Salkantay Trek and the Lares Trek, provide varied scenery and cultural experiences. If trekking is not your thing, you may take a picturesque train trip directly from Cusco or the Sacred Valley to Aguas Calientes, the gateway town to Machu Picchu.

4. Obtain Permits and Tickets: If you intend to trek the Inca Trail, you must first obtain permits, which are in limited supply and must be obtained well in advance. Purchasing tickets and admission permits to Machu Picchu for other climbs or train journeys can normally be done online or through authorized travel agencies. It is best to schedule them as soon as possible in order to guarantee your preferred dates.

5. Consider Acclimatization: Machu Picchu is located at a high altitude of around 2,430 meters (7,972 feet). It is recommended that you spend a few days acclimatizing in Cusco or the Sacred Valley before visiting Machu Picchu to avoid altitude sickness. Take it easy, drink plenty of water, and avoid strenuous physical activity during the first few days to give your body time to acclimate.

6. Pack wisely: Be prepared for a variety of weather conditions. Pack light, wicking clothing, suitable walking shoes, a rain jacket, sunscreen, a hat, and bug repellent. Don't forget to include basics like a

reusable water bottle, a daypack, and any prescriptions you may require.

7. Hiring a professional guide or participating in a guided tour can enhance your experience at Machu Picchu. They can provide historical and cultural insights help you navigate the intricate site, and provide you insider information. Consider supporting local tour companies and guides to help the region's long-term prosperity.

8. Beyond Machu Picchu: While Machu Picchu is clearly the main draw, the region is home to a plethora of other fascinating sights and activities. Consider visiting the Sacred Valley, which contains old Inca ruins, traditional marketplaces, and gorgeous towns such as Ollantaytambo and Pisac.

9. Respect and Preserve: Machu Picchu is a UNESCO World Heritage Site, and it is critical to preserve and sustain it. Follow the authorities' guidelines, avoid trash, and be respectful of the vulnerable ecosystem. Leave only footprints and bring back memories to last a lifetime.

You can arrange a wonderful trip to Machu Picchu by following these steps and planning ahead of time. Allow yourself to be immersed in this historic wonderland's natural beauty and cultural wealth.

CHAPTER TWO

Getting Ready for Your Journey

A trip to Machu Picchu necessitates precise planning in order to maximize your experience. Here are some helpful hints to get you ready for your adventure:

1. Walking, hiking, and exploring difficult terrain are all part of the experience of Machu Picchu and its surrounding locations. To truly enjoy your trip, you must be in good physical condition. Prior to your journey, engage in regular exercise and activities that will help you build endurance and stamina. Consult your healthcare provider as well to ensure you are suitable for high-altitude travel.

2. Acclimatization: Because Machu Picchu is located at a high altitude, acclimatization is essential to avoid altitude sickness. Spend a few days in Cusco or the Sacred Valley before visiting Machu Picchu to allow your body to gradually acclimate to the altitude. Take it easy the first several days, drink

plenty of water, and avoid strenuous physical activity.

3. Documentation Required: Make sure you have all of the appropriate documentation for your trip. This includes a valid passport (valid for at least six months), any necessary visas, and duplicates of vital documents such as your passport, travel insurance, and permits. Store both physical and digital copies in a safe location.

4. Travel Insurance: Get comprehensive travel insurance that covers medical emergencies, trip cancellation or interruption, and lost or stolen possessions. Check to see if your policy covers high-altitude activities like trekking, if appropriate.

5. Immunizations and Health Precautions: Consult a medical provider about recommended immunizations for Peru travel. Hepatitis A and B, typhoid, and tetanus immunizations are all prevalent. Additionally, protect yourself against mosquito bites by using insect repellent and wearing long sleeves and pants, especially if you live

in an area where mosquito-borne diseases such as dengue or Zika are a danger.

6. Pack sensibly; taking in mind the weather and activities you'll be participating in. Comfortable walking shoes, breathable and layered clothing, a hat, sunglasses, sunscreen, a reusable water bottle, a daypack, a rain jacket, and basic first aid supplies are all recommended. Don't forget to bring any necessary prescriptions and toiletries.

7. Currency and Finances: The Peruvian Sol (PEN) is the country's official currency. It's a good idea to have some local cash on hand for little purchases and tips. Inform your bank and credit card firms of your travel plans to avoid problems accessing funds or potential card blocking. Also, keep extra cash in tiny denominations on hand in case card payment is not feasible.

8. Check with your cell phone service provider about international roaming choices and prices. Consider acquiring a local SIM card upon arrival for inexpensive communication during your stay. Wi-Fi

is usually offered in hotels and several cafes, but connectivity in outlying regions may be limited.

9. Learn Basic Spanish: While it is not required, knowing a few basic Spanish phrases can help you engage with locals and make your travel experience more enjoyable. Learn standard greetings, courteous expressions, and basic words for ordering meals or requesting directions.

10. Cultural Etiquette: To show respect for the local culture, become acquainted with local customs and etiquette. Learn a few basic phrases in Spanish, observe clothing regulations at sacred locations, and obtain permission before photographing people or their belongings.

By following these preparation measures, you will be more prepared to face the hardships, embrace the wonders, and make enduring experiences at Machu Picchu. Take in every detail of your experience in this wonderful part of the world.

Documentation and Visa Requirements

Before beginning your adventure to Machu Picchu, it is critical to become acquainted with the necessary travel paperwork and visas for entry into Peru. Here's what you should know:

1. Passport: All overseas tourists entering Peru must have a valid passport. Verify that the passport you're using is valid for at least six months after the date of your planned travel. Examine its condition to ensure that there is no damage or missing pages.

2. Visa Requirements: Visa requirements for Peru vary by nationality. Many countries' citizens, including those from the United States, Canada, the European Union, Australia, and New Zealand, can enter Peru as tourists without a visa for stays of up to 183 days. However, it is always a good idea to contact the Peruvian consulate or embassy in your country to confirm the precise visa requirements based on your nationality.

3. Tourist Card (Tambo): You will be given a tourist card, commonly known as a Tambo card, upon your

31

arrival in Peru. This card is free to get and is required for admission into the nation. Fill out the essential information and keep the card safe during your stay. You could be requested to show it as you leave.

4. Forms for Immigration and Customs: Upon arriving in Peru, you will be required to fill out an immigration form, which is normally issued on the plane or at the airport. This form contains personal information as well as information regarding your stay. You may also be needed to complete a customs declaration form, declaring any items of value or banned products that you are bringing into the nation.

5. Proof of Return or Onward Travel: When entering Peru, it is suggested that you have proof of return or onward travel. This can be in the form of a return flight ticket or a confirmed itinerary out of Peru. Immigration officers may request this information to ensure that you intend to depart the country within the time limit.

6. Yellow Fever Vaccination: While not required for admission into Peru, a yellow fever vaccination certificate is required if you are arriving from a country where yellow fever transmission is possible. Check to see if your home country or any nations you've recently visited are on the list of countries that require the immunization. It is best to consult a healthcare practitioner about any necessary immunizations or health precautions for your travel.

7. Travel Insurance: Although not a requirement for visiting Machu Picchu, having comprehensive travel insurance is highly advised. Make sure your policy covers medical emergencies, trip cancellation or interruption, and any adventure activities like high-altitude treks you want to participate in.

Remember to verify the most recent visa and travel document requirements well in advance of your trip, since restrictions are subject to change. For the most up-to-date information particular to your nationality, always contact the Peruvian embassy or consulate in your country.

You'll be well-prepared for a smooth and hassle-free entry into Peru and a genuinely unforgettable visit to Machu Picchu if you make sure you have the proper travel documents and meet the visa requirements.

Considerations Regarding Health and Safety

When visiting Machu Picchu, it is critical to prioritize your health and safety. Outlined are some important facts to remember:

1. Consult a Healthcare expert: Prior to your journey, make an appointment with a healthcare expert, preferably one who specializes in travel medicine. Discuss your travel intentions, including any pre-existing medical conditions, and ask about required vaccinations, altitude sickness preventive drugs, and general health advice for your trip.

2. Acclimatization to height: Machu Picchu is located at a high height, and altitude sickness might affect

some visitors. Spend a few days in Cusco or the Sacred Valley before ascending to Machu Picchu to reduce your risk. Allow your body to acclimatize gradually by taking it easy upon arrival, drinking plenty of water, and avoiding strenuous physical activity during the first several days.

3. Hydration and Sun Protection: Drink plenty of water throughout your vacation to stay hydrated, especially in high-altitude situations. Wear a hat and use high-SPF sunscreen to protect yourself from the sun's rays, which can be more fierce at higher altitudes.

4. Insect Protection: Mosquitoes may be present in some locations of Peru, particularly the Amazon jungle. Use insect repellent, wear long sleeves and pants, and sleep under mosquito nets if required to protect you. If you plan to travel malaria-risk areas, speak with a healthcare practitioner about malaria prevention.

5. Food and Water Safety: It is critical to take precautions with food and water while traveling in Peru. Use bottled water or water purification

procedures such as boiling, filtering, or water purification pills instead. Avoid street food and choose establishments with adequate cleanliness practices. Before eating, wash your hands regularly or use hand sanitizer.

6. Travel Insurance: It is critical to have comprehensive travel insurance that covers medical crises, trip cancellation or interruption, and emergency evacuation. Ascertain that your policy covers high-altitude activities including trekking, if relevant.

7. Trekking Safety: If you want to hike to Machu Picchu, find a trustworthy tour operator who follows safety requirements. Make sure you have the necessary equipment, such as solid footwear, rain gear, and layers for changeable weather situations. Follow your guide's directions, stay on approved trails, and be aware of your physical limitations.

8. Personal Safety: While Peru is typically a safe country for visitors, it is always prudent to exercise cautious. Keep your stuff secure and be attentive of your surroundings, especially in crowded situations.

Avoid openly exhibiting expensive objects and instead carry vital documents and cash in a money belt or a lockable bag.

9. Respect Local cultures: Become acquainted with Peruvian cultures and traditions. Respect sacred sites, adhere to dress requirements in religious settings, and obtain permission before photographing individuals or their belongings. Engage in polite conversation with locals and acquire a few basic Spanish phrases to facilitate communication.

10. Stay Informed: Stay up to current on travel warnings and other regional safety information. To receive travel warnings or notifications throughout your stay, register with your embassy or consulate.

Packing Requirements

When packing for your vacation to Machu Picchu, make sure you have everything you need to have a comfortable and happy experience. Consider the following packing essentials:

1. Pack lightweight, moisture-wicking apparel that can be layered. Trekking requires comfortable walking shoes or hiking boots with sufficient traction. Remember to bring socks, underwear, and sleepwear. Warmer clothes, such as a fleece jacket or a light down jacket, may be required depending on the season.

2. Rain Gear: Regardless of the season, surprise rain showers can occur in Machu Picchu and the surrounding areas. To keep dry, bring a waterproof or water-resistant jacket or poncho. Consider including a rain cover in your backpack.

3. Daypack: When touring Machu Picchu and its surroundings, a modest daypack is essential for carrying your daily requirements. Choose a backpack that is lightweight and comfortable, with enough space to contain your water bottle, snacks, camera, sunscreen, and other personal goods.

4. Travel paperwork: Keep all of your travel paperwork organized and easy to find. This comprises your passport, visa (if necessary), travel insurance information, copies of crucial documents

such as your passport and permits, and any vaccination certificates that may be required.

5. Medications: If you take prescription medications, be sure you have enough for the duration of your vacation. Consider bringing a small first aid kit stocked with essentials such as bandages, antibacterial ointment, pain medicines, and any personal medications or therapies tailored to your specific needs.

6. Sun Protection: Because the sun's rays can be harsh at higher altitudes, bring sunscreen with a high SPF and consider packing a hat and sunglasses. SPF lip balm is also advised.

7. Insect Repellent: Depending on your schedule and activities, it's a good idea to bring insect repellent to protect yourself from mosquitoes and other insects, especially if you plan to visit locations where mosquito-borne diseases are prevalent.

Reusable Water Bottle: It is critical to stay hydrated, especially at high elevations. Pack a reusable water bottle to fill and carry with you all day. To refill your bottle, use purified or bottled water.

8. Snacks: Bring some lightweight, non-perishable snacks with you, such as energy bars, trail mix, or dried fruits, to keep you energized while exploring. These can be useful, especially on lengthy trips or walks.

9. Electronics: Don't forget to bring your camera or smartphone to capture the breathtaking scenery and memories of your trip. Bring the chargers, adapters, and power banks you'll need to keep your gadgets charged throughout your journey.

10. Miscellaneous: Pack a tiny travel towel, a headlamp or flashlight, a pocket-sized umbrella, a travel adapter, a money belt or secure pouch for your belongings, and a comfy neck pillow for long flights.

Remember to pack light and carry only what you truly require. Check the weather prediction for the period of your visit as well, and adapt your packing appropriately. You'll be ready to embrace the adventure and beauty of Machu Picchu if you're well-prepared and bring the necessities.

Choosing the Best Season to Visit

When to visit Machu Picchu is a crucial factor to guarantee you get the greatest experience possible. Here are some things to consider while deciding on the best time to travel:

1. Weather: The climate of Machu Picchu is influenced by its high altitude and proximity to the equator. The dry season, from May through October, is typically regarded as the ideal time to visit. You should expect sunny sky, fewer possibilities of rain, and nice daytime temperatures throughout this time. More rain falls during the rainy season, which lasts from November to April, notably in January and February. Even during the rainy season, though, there are frequent intervals of sunshine, and the scenery becomes rich and vivid.

2. Crowds: Because Machu Picchu is a popular tourist attraction, you should organize your visit

accordingly. The peak tourist season corresponds to the dry season, especially from June to August. Expect to see more people during this season, especially at famous vistas and during peak visitation hours. If you prefer a more tranquil experience, go during the shoulder seasons of May and September/October, when the weather is still pleasant and the people are slightly lower.

3. Permit Availability: If you intend to hike the famous Inca Trail to Machu Picchu, you should check the availability of permits. The Inca Trail has a daily limit of people, and permits sometimes sell out months in advance, especially during high season. To ensure that your preferred trekking dates are available, it is best to book your permits well in advance.

4. Peru is well-known for its lively festivals and cultural events. If you want to learn about local traditions and celebrations, look up the dates of festivals like Inti Raymi (June 24th) and Virgen del Carmen (July 15th), which are held in the Cusco region. Keep in mind that while these events may

draw greater crowds, they provide a one-of-a-kind cultural experience.

5. Personal Preferences: When deciding when to visit, consider your own preferences and priorities. Are you more concerned with pleasant weather, less crowds, or attending a certain cultural event? Consider what is most important to you and plan your visit appropriately.

6. Accessibility: It is crucial to note that Machu Picchu is open all year, regardless of weather. However, any potential travel difficulties during the rainy season, such as landslides or temporary trail closures, should be considered. Keep up with weather forecasts and any local government alerts.

CHAPTER THREE

How to Get to Machu Picchu

Getting to Machu Picchu is a thrilling part of your journey. Here are the important steps to take and transportation choices to think about:

1. Arriving in Cusco: Most visitors begin their trek to Machu Picchu in Cusco, the ancient site's gateway city. Cusco's Alejandro Velasco Astete International Airport handles both domestic and international aircraft. From there, you can either take the train or hike the Inca Trail to Machu Picchu.

2. By Train: The most popular mode of transportation to Machu Picchu is by train. PeruRail and Inca Rail are the two primary train companies in Peru. The railway travels from Cusco or the Sacred Valley (Ollantaytambo) to Aguas Calientes, the settlement at the foot of Machu Picchu. The train journey provides breathtaking views of the Andean countryside, and you may select from a variety of

classes and amenities to suit your interests and budget.

3. Hiking the Inca Trail: Hiking the Inca Trail is a popular alternative for people looking for a more adventurous and immersive experience. This four-day walk takes you through stunning mountain landscapes, old Inca sites, and a variety of habitats. Permits are required to hike the Inca Trail, and it is critical to reserve ahead of time because spots can fill up rapidly, especially during peak season. Prepare for physically hard terrain and high altitude, and think about hiring a trustworthy trip operator to provide guides, equipment, and sleeping arrangements.

4. Alternative Trekking Routes: If Inca Trail permits are unavailable or you prefer a different trekking experience, alternative routes to Machu Picchu include the Salkantay Trek, Lares Trek, and Choquequirao Trek. These itineraries provide unusual scenery, cultural contacts, and the opportunity to visit lesser-known Inca sites.

5. Aguas Calientes to Machu Picchu: The final phase of your journey to Machu Picchu begins when you arrive in Aguas Calientes. You may take a shuttle bus from town to the entrance to Machu Picchu, which weaves its way up the rocky mountainside. The bus travel takes about 30 minutes. For the more daring and physically capable, you can climb up to Machu Picchu from Aguas Calientes. The hike, known as the "Hiram Bingham" or "Inca Trail," is a strenuous uphill climb that takes approximately 1-2 hours.

Remember to plan ahead of time for transportation and permits, especially during high season. Be prepared for weather fluctuations and pack appropriately. It's also a good idea to hire a qualified guide who can enrich your experience by explaining the history and significance of Machu Picchu.

Getting to Machu Picchu is an exciting journey that will take you to one of the world's most spectacular archaeological monuments. Embrace the journey, take in the amazing vistas, and ready to be awestruck by Machu Picchu's beauty.

Lima Peru Arrival

Welcome to Lima, Peru's capital city! Prepare to be immersed in a colorful blend of history, culture, and culinary delights when you arrive in Lima. Here's what to expect when you arrive:

1. Jorge Chávez International Airport: You'll land in Callao, just outside Lima, at Jorge Chávez International Airport. This contemporary airport provides a variety of services, such as currency exchange, ATMs, vehicle rental services, and stores. Take a few moments to become acquainted with the airport layout and obtain any relevant information or maps.

2. Immigration and Customs: After disembarking from the plane, you will go through immigration. Prepare your passport, completed immigration forms (if necessary), and necessary travel documentation. After passing through immigration,

take your luggage to the customs section. Prepare to declare any products or items that customs regulations require.

3. Ground Transportation: There are various options for getting from the airport to your hotel in Lima. Cabs are widely available, although it is best to use authorized taxi services or pre-booked cabs to assure safety and fair pricing. Some hotels also offer airport shuttle services, so check to see if your hotel provides this option. In Lima, ride-hailing services such as Uber are also available.

4. Lima Exploration: As you settle into Lima, you'll discover a city rich in history, architecture, and a diverse food scene. Consider visiting Lima's historic city, a UNESCO World Heritage Site, which features spectacular colonial architecture such as the famed Plaza Mayor (Main Square), the Cathedral of Lima, and the Government Palace. Take a stroll through the picturesque streets and eat delicious Peruvian food at one of the many restaurants and cafés.

5. Miraflores and Barranco: Miraflores and Barranco are two popular districts to visit in Lima. Miraflores

has beautiful seaside vistas, parks, shopping malls, and a bustling culinary scene. Take a walk along the Malecón (coastal promenade) for spectacular views of the Pacific Ocean. Barranco, noted for its bohemian vibe, with colorful streets, art galleries, and a thriving nightlife. Explore the local art culture and don't miss the renowned Puente de los Suspiros (Bridge of Sighs).

6. Gastronomic Delights: Lima is known as one of the world's culinary capitals. Indulge in a culinary adventure and sample Peruvian cuisine, which combines indigenous, Spanish, African, and Asian influences. Try ceviche, a delectable dish of raw fish or seafood marinated in citrus juices, or anticuchos, grilled marinated meat skewers. Visit local markets like Mercado Surquillo or Mercado de Magdalena to get a taste of the local cuisine.

While Lima is a great experience, it is critical to be cautious about your safety. Avoid secluded regions at night, keep an eye on your possessions, and only use approved taxis or ride-hailing services. Keep up to date on any travel advisories or safety advice issued for the city.

Lima serves as the starting point for a memorable adventure around Peru. Soak in the city's dynamic energy, revel in its gastronomic delights, and experience Lima's distinct blend of history and modernity. Have a wonderful day in the City of Kings!

Cusco Transportation Options

After arriving in Lima, you'll take an unforgettable journey to Cusco, the gateway city to Machu Picchu. Here are the several modes of transportation accessible to reach this historic and culturally significant location:

1. Domestic Flights: Flying from Lima to Cusco is the most convenient and time-efficient option. Several airlines fly regularly between Lima's Jorge Chávez International Airport and Cusco's Alejandro Velasco Astete International Airport. The journey lasts about an hour and provides breathtaking aerial views of

the Peruvian terrain. It's essential to book your flights ahead of time to get the greatest deals.

2. Overland Bus Travel: If you want a more picturesque and cost-effective route, you can travel by bus from Lima to Cusco. On this route, several bus companies offer luxurious and well-equipped buses. The voyage takes between 20 and 24 hours, depending on the route and stops. Some buses provide several degrees of service, such as reclining seats, onboard entertainment, and food. It is best to go with a reputed bus operator that promotes safety and comfort.

3. Train Journeys: There are train choices from Lima to Cusco for travelers looking for a unique and scenic experience. Please keep in mind that there is no direct train service between the two cities. You'd have to take a combination of trains and buses instead. Typically, the voyage begins with a train from Lima to Huancayo, a lovely city in Peru's highlands, and then continues by bus or train to Cusco. This alternative takes more time, but it allows

you to see spectacular mountain views and visit lesser-known sites.

4. Combination of Bus and rail: Another alternative for getting to Cusco is to combine bus and rail travel. Take a bus from Lima to Arequipa, which is famed for its beautiful colonial architecture and proximity to the Colca Canyon. You can next enjoy a picturesque train ride to Cusco from Arequipa. This option allows you to break up the journey and see two amazing places along the route.

Whatever mode of transportation you use, it is critical to plan your route ahead of time. Think about things like trip time, affordability, comfort, and personal preferences. Keep in mind that airline availability might fluctuate, especially during peak travel seasons, so it's best to book your flights or bus/train tickets ahead of time.

Prepare to be charmed by Cusco's rich history, Inca ruins, and colorful culture when you go there. From Cusco, you have several alternatives for getting to Machu Picchu, including taking the train, climbing the Inca Trail, or using alternate trekking paths. As you explore Peru's marvels, embrace the adventure and ready for an amazing experience.

Choosing the Best Machu Picchu Route

When it comes to getting to Machu Picchu, there are various options to select, each with its own distinct experience. Here are the primary choices for determining the optimal route for your journey:

1. The Classic Inca Trail is the most well-known and popular trekking route to Machu Picchu. This well-known trek takes you on a four-day adventure through breathtaking Andean scenery, ancient Inca sites, and various ecosystems. You'll walk in the footsteps of the Incas, passing through the spectacular Sun Gate to see Machu Picchu at daybreak. The Classic Inca Trail requires a permit and is limited to a certain number of tourists each day, so plan ahead of time.

2. Alternative Trekking Routes: If permits for the Classic Inca Trail are unavailable, or if you prefer a less crowded trekking experience, there are other

routes to Machu Picchu that are equally charming and beautiful. The Salkantay Trek, Lares Trek, and Choquequirao Trek are all popular alternatives. These paths take you through breathtaking scenery, secluded Andean settlements, and lesser-known Inca sites. Each alternate route has a different amount of difficulty and duration, so do your homework and pick the one that best meets your preferences and fitness level.

3. Hiram Bingham Train: The Hiram Bingham train is a fantastic alternative for those looking for a more pleasant and luxury experience. This railway, named for the American explorer who explored Machu Picchu, provides an upscale experience with exquisite carriages, gourmet food, live music, and panoramic windows that reflect the magnificent grandeur of the Urubamba River Valley. The Hiram Bingham train leaves Cusco and travels directly to Aguas Calientes, the village at the foot of Machu Picchu.

4. The Expedition train is a wonderful alternative if you prefer a more economical train option. This

PeruRail train provides comfortable seating, huge windows, and a relaxing ambiance. It offers a beautiful route from Cusco or the Sacred Valley (Ollantaytambo) to Aguas Calientes. The Expedition train allows you to take in the scenery and make the most of your travel time.

If trekking isn't your thing, you may still experience the enchantment of Machu Picchu by taking a bus and hiking combination. You may take a shuttle bus from Aguas Calientes to the entrance to Machu Picchu, which weaves its way up the steep mountainside. Once inside, you may walk about the ancient ruins, taking in the breathtaking architecture and panoramic vistas. This alternative allows you to immerse yourself in Machu Picchu's historical value without the physical difficulties of a multi-day journey.

Consider your fitness level, preferred level of comfort, time available, and preference for isolation or camaraderie while deciding on the best route to Machu Picchu. The trek to Machu Picchu is an adventure of a lifetime, regardless of whatever route you take. As you set foot in one of the world's most amazing sites, prepare to be enchanted by the beauty and mystery of this ancient treasure.

Trekking vs. Train: Which is Better for You?

One essential decision to make when arranging a trip to Machu Picchu is whether to trek or take the train. Both alternatives provide distinct experiences, so it's critical to examine your preferences, physical fitness, time limits, and desired level of adventure. Let's examine the trekking and rail choices to see which is best for you:

1. Machu Picchu Trekking:

i. Immersive encounter: Trekking to Machu Picchu, whether through the Classic Inca Trail or other routes, provides a completely immersive encounter. You'll be able to hike through breathtaking scenery, cross mountain passes, see historic Inca ruins, and connect with nature. Trekking allows you to immerse yourself in the Andean scenery and the trail's challenges in a more close and personal way.

ii. Physical Demand: The trek to Machu Picchu necessitates a certain level of physical fitness and endurance. The paths can be difficult to navigate, with steep ascents and descents and high heights. The physical difficulty, on the other hand, may be extremely rewarding, as it forces you out of your comfort zone and provides a sense of success once reaching Machu Picchu. Before beginning on a trekking journey, it is critical to fully train and prepare.

iii. The Classic Inca Trail and several alternate routes require permits, and the number of daily tourists is limited. Booking ahead of time is essential, especially for the Classic Inca Trail, as permits might sell out rapidly. Trekking is a terrific option if you prefer a more private and off-the-beaten-path experience.

2. Getting to Machu Picchu by Train:

i. Comfort and Convenience: Taking the train to Machu Picchu is a more comfortable and convenient choice, particularly for those who prefer to avoid rigorous physical exercise. The train offers a relaxing ride with comfortable seating, huge windows to admire the scenery, and services including onboard beverages and entertainment.

ii. Time-saving: Trekking to Machu Picchu takes many days, whereas riding the train is a faster choice. The train ride from Cusco or the Sacred Valley to Aguas Calientes, the village at the base of Machu Picchu, is only a few hours long, giving you more time to see the ruins or participate in other activities.

iii. Spectacular Scenery: While trekking allows you to get up close and personal with nature, taking the train allows you to see the Peruvian environment from a different perspective. The train will take you through the Andean mountains and along the Urubamba River, providing stunning views of the region's splendor.

iv. Accessibility: The rail alternative is more accessible to a broader range of people, including those with physical disabilities or limited time. It's a good option for families, seniors, or anyone who desires a more calm and accessible ride.

The decision between trekking and taking the train to Machu Picchu is influenced by your personal tastes, physical condition, available time, and the type of experience you seek. Trekking can be a transforming trip if you appreciate a physical challenge, want a deeper connection with nature, and have the time. If you prefer comfort, convenience, and a faster ride, the train is a scenic and delightful option. Whatever path you take, Machu Picchu will leave you speechless with its timeless beauty and historical significance.

CHAPTER FOUR

Visiting Cusco

Cusco, the gateway to Machu Picchu, is a city rich in history, culture, and spectacular natural beauty. This old Inca Empire capital in the Peruvian Andes provides a compelling blend of ancient ruins, colonial architecture, and thriving local culture. Here's a taste of what to anticipate when visiting Cusco:

1. Plaza de Armas: Begin your trip with the Plaza de Armas, Cusco's central square. This bustling city is surrounded by beautiful colonial architecture, such as the Cusco Cathedral and the Church of the Society of Jesus. Take some time to observe the complex architecture, people-watch, and enjoy the bustling environment. The plaza is also an excellent location for purchasing local crafts, artwork, and souvenirs.

2. Sacsayhuaman: The historic fortification of Sacsayhuaman is located just outside of Cusco. This

massive archaeological site features amazing stone walls and breathtaking views of Cusco. Explore the magnificent masonry and marvel at the Incas' engineering genius. If you come during the Inti Raymi celebration in June, you'll be able to see colorful reenactments of Inca ceremonies here.

3. Qorikancha: Learn about the Inca Empire's intriguing history at Qorikancha, commonly known as the Temple of the Sun. This was the Incas' most important holy place, and its walls were previously decorated with gold and valuable stones. While the Spanish conquistadors demolished much of the temple, parts of the original edifice can still be seen today in the Santo Domingo Church that sits on the site.

4. Take a stroll through the bohemian San Blas area, which is noted for its narrow cobblestone lanes, artisan workshops, and pleasant ambience. Many excellent local artists, painters, and jewelry makers call this creative sector home. Explore the charming stores and art galleries, and take in the scenic views of the city from the San Blas viewpoint.

5. Museums: Several museums in Cusco provide insights into the region's rich history and culture. The Museo de Arte Precolombino holds an impressive collection of pre-Columbian antiquities, and the Museo Inka houses an extensive collection of Inca artifacts and displays. The Centro de Textiles Tradicionales, where you may learn about traditional Andean textile techniques, and the Museo de Historia Regional, which dives into the history of Cusco and the surrounding region, are two other noteworthy museums.

6. Gastronomic Delights: The gastronomic scene in Cusco is a fascinating combination of traditional Andean flavors and international influences. Enjoy regional specialties like as ceviche, alpaca steak, and quinoa soup. To aid with altitude acclimatization, drink a cup of mate de coca (coca tea). Explore the rich colors and flavors of fresh vegetables, spices, and street food at local markets like San Pedro Market.

Cusco is noted for its lively festivals and celebrations that combine traditional Inca customs with Catholic influences. If you're in Cusco around Inti Raymi (Sun Festival) in June or Corpus Christi in June, you'll see colorful processions, music, dance, and cultural events that highlight the region's rich legacy.

Cusco has an enthralling combination of history, culture, and natural beauty that will leave you speechless. Take your time.

Exploring the Historic District

Cusco's old center is a UNESCO World Heritage site that is rich in history, architecture, and cultural significance. Wander around the city's small streets and discover its unique landmarks to immerse yourself in its rich tapestry. Here are some of the highlights of the historic district:

1. Cusco Cathedral: The Cusco Cathedral, which dominates the Plaza de Armas, is a beautiful example of Spanish colonial architecture. Step inside to enjoy its opulence, magnificent altars, and stunning artwork. Don't miss Marcos Zapata's Last

Supper artwork, which has a particularly Andean touch with a cuy (guinea pig) on the table.

2. The Church of the Society of Jesus (Iglesia de la Compaa de Jess) is a masterpiece of baroque architecture located near the Plaza de Armas. Its façade is beautifully carved with religious symbols, and its inside is lavishly decorated with gold leaf. Take a moment to admire the intricate craftsmanship and the beautiful San Ignacio Chapel.

3. San Pedro Market: At the San Pedro Market, you may immerse yourself in the vibrant local culture. This bustling market is a sensory delight, overflowing with vibrant fruits, veggies, spices, and handicrafts. Try exotic fruits, local delicacies, and chat with pleasant merchants. It's a terrific spot to learn about Cusqueos' daily lives and purchase for unusual items.

4. Hatunrumiyoc Street: Take a stroll down Hatunrumiyoc Street, which is notable for its Inca walls. As you view the precisely aligned stones without any mortar, admire the Incas' precision and engineering prowess. The Twelve-Angle Stone, an

excellent example of Inca stonework that blends in with nearby stones, is the street's showpiece.

5. Museo de Arte Precolombino (Museum of Pre-Columbian Art): This museum exhibits an excellent collection of pre-Columbian art and is housed in a beautifully restored colonial home. Admire the beautiful ceramics, textiles, and goldwork that provide insights into the various cultures that flourished in Peru prior to the advent of the Spaniards.

6. Plaza San Blas: A bohemian square filled with art galleries, artisan workshops, and small cafés, Plaza San Blas is a must-see. Admire the gorgeous San Blas Church, which is noted for its elaborate wood-carved pulpit, and soak up the creative spirit.

7. Qurikancha (Temple of the Sun): Dive into ancient Inca culture at Qurikancha, one of the Inca Empire's most important temples. Although the Spanish demolished much of the temple, you may still see vestiges of its grandeur and admire the amazing stone masonry. The site also features a small

museum that provides additional information about Inca rites and traditions.

Exploring Cusco's ancient core is like going back in time, where the Inca Empire's ruins coexist with the Spanish colonial legacy. Allow yourself to be mesmerized by the magnificent architecture, the intriguing history behind each monument, and the vivid energy that pervades the streets. It's an event that will leave you with a greater respect for this amazing city's rich cultural legacy.

Exploring Sacsayhuaman and Other Inca Ruins

A visit to the Incan ruins is a necessity when seeing Cusco and its surroundings. These archaeological sites provide insight into the Inca civilization's outstanding architectural abilities and spiritual beliefs. Here are some noteworthy Incan ruins to visit:

1. Sacsayhuaman: Located just outside of Cusco, Sacsayhuaman is a magnificent fortification and ceremonial complex. Admire the gigantic stone walls erected with great accuracy, some of which weigh more than 100 tons. Explore the zigzagging fortifications, underground passages, and the Inti Watana, an astronomical observatory made of stone. Enjoy panoramic views of Cusco and the surrounding mountains from the spot.

2. Pisac: Located in the Sacred Valley, Pisac is a large archaeological site including terraces, temples, and residential districts. The ruins are set on a mountainside and provide stunning views of the valley below. Explore the artistically carved stone monuments, such as the Intihuatana (a sundial-like stone), and envision life in this old Inca settlement.

3. Ollantaytambo: Known as the "Living Inca City," Ollantaytambo is a well-preserved town with original Inca urban layout. The site is dominated by the castle of Ollantaytambo, which features massive stone terraces and spectacular monoliths. Climb the steep stone steps to the summit for panoramic

views of the town and neighboring mountains. Ollantaytambo is also the starting point for the train ride to Machu Picchu.

4. Moray: Explore the fascinating circular terraces of Moray, an agricultural laboratory thought to have been used by the Incas for crop research. The terraces, which are laid out in concentric circles, provide a microclimate that allowed the Incas to cultivate crops at different temperatures. Walk down into the terraces to experience the special spirit of this sacred location.

5. Tipón: Tipón is a series of agricultural terraces, fountains, and irrigation channels located in the countryside near Cusco. It was a crucial location for water management and agricultural experiments. Admire the complex stone channels and explore the terraces while admiring the Inca engineering brilliance.

6. Choquequirao: A trek to Choquequirao is a wonderful experience for the more adventurous traveler. This distant archaeological site, known as the "sister city" of Machu Picchu, is still being

excavated. Trek across difficult terrain to see spectacular terraces, ceremonial platforms, and breathtaking vistas of the surrounding mountains.

Imagine the thriving cities, vivid rites, and deep spiritual relationships that once thrived within these Incan ruins as you visit them. Listen to the whispers of history and wonder at the Inca civilization's architectural accomplishments. Each location provides a different perspective on their culture and will leave you in awe of their great legacy.

Discovering About the Local Culture and Cuisine

Cusco is more than just old ruins; it's also a thriving center of culture and culinary pleasures. Immerse yourself in local traditions, connect with friendly locals, and delight your taste buds with Cusco's distinctive delicacies. Here's how you may immerse yourself in the local culture and cuisine:

1. Attend a Traditional ritual: Cusco is firmly ingrained in its Inca legacy, and attending a traditional ritual is an excellent way to immerse you in the local culture. Look for celebrations or rituals that pay honor to the Inca gods and commemorate the region's rich past. The Inti Raymi celebration, held in June, is especially impressive, with colorful processions and traditional entertainment.

2. Step into the vibrant ambiance of the San Pedro Market, where the sights, sounds, and fragrances will captivate your senses. This lively market is a foodie's paradise and a terrific place to try local products, snacks, and traditional cuisine. Interact with vendors, learn about unusual ingredients, and sample Peruvian delicacies such as ceviche, anticuchos (grilled skewers), and rocoto relleno (stuffed spicy peppers).

3. Take a Cooking Class: Learn more about Peruvian cuisine by enrolling in a cooking class in Cusco. Learn how to make classic foods like lomo saltado (stir-fried beef), causa (potato-based dish), and aji de gallina (creamy chicken stew). Discover the

varied flavors of Peruvian ingredients and gain insight into centuries-old culinary traditions.

4. Enjoy Local Festivals: Cusco is well-known for its lively festivals, which feature traditional music, dancing, and costumes. Immerse yourself in the celebrations if you happen to visit during a festival, such as Corpus Christi or the Festival of the Sun. Join the bustling street processions, see traditional dances, and feel the residents' happy attitude as they celebrate their cultural heritage.

5. Visit Artisan Workshops: Cusco is a haven for creative artists who use traditional techniques to create stunning products. Explore the streets of San Blas, which is known for its artisan workshops, and see expert craftsmen at work. Admire the elaborate weavings, silver jewelry, and bright paintings that depict Andean culture.

6. Try Pisco and Cusquea Beer: No trip to Cusco is complete without sampling the local beverages. Try Pisco, Peru's national liquor distilled from grapes and available in a variety of tastes. Try a Pisco tasting to find your favorite kind. Enjoy a crisp

Cusquea beer, a popular local brew that pairs wonderfully with the Andean climate.

7. Participate in Community Tourism: Consider taking part in community-based tourism programs that allow you to engage with local communities while also contributing to their long-term development. Home stays, weaving workshops, and agricultural experiences not only give an authentic cultural interaction but also help to sustain the livelihoods of local residents.

Cusco is a city that is proud of its cultural past, providing a plethora of experiences that highlight its history, traditions, and flavors. You'll create unique experiences that genuinely capture the essence of Cusco by immersing yourself in the local culture and relishing the different cuisine offers.

Altitude Acclimatization

Acclimatizing to the high altitude is an important part of visiting Cusco. Cusco's elevation of about 3,400 meters (11,150 feet) above sea level might be taxing on your body if you are not sufficiently prepared. Here are some pointers to help you adjust to and enjoy your visit to this gorgeous Andean city:

1. Allow your body to acclimate to the altitude by taking it easy for the first couple of days. Avoid hard activities and make time for rest. Cusco's small alleyways and attractive plazas are ideal for leisurely strolls where you can soak up the atmosphere without exerting yourself.

2. Stay Hydrated: To stay hydrated and combat the effects of altitude, drink plenty of water. Excessive alcohol consumption and caffeinated beverages should be avoided since they might contribute to dehydration. Coca tea, a traditional local treatment produced from coca leaves, is frequently recommended to help relieve the symptoms of altitude sickness.

3. Plan your trip to include moderate ascents to higher altitudes if possible. For example, because it is at a lower level, you can visit the Sacred Valley before travelling to Cusco. This allows your body to gradually acclimate to the higher altitude.

4. Medication: Before your travel, consult with your healthcare provider about the potential of taking medication to assist avoid or lessen altitude sickness symptoms. Acetazolamide, often known as Diamox, is a medicine that is occasionally used for this reason. However, it is critical to seek tailored guidance from a medical practitioner.

5. Light Meals: Choose light, easy-to-digest meals over hefty meals, which can make you feel more uncomfortable at higher altitudes. Choose carbohydrate-rich diets and avoid items high in fat and protein. Local meals such as quinoa soup or grilled fish might provide nourishment without straining your digestive system.

6. Restful Sleep: Adequate rest is essential for acclimatization. Rest easy at night and give yourself plenty of time to sleep and recover. Many Cusco hotels have rooms with oxygen supplementation, which can help relieve symptoms and enhance sleep quality.

7. Pay Attention to Your Body: Pay attention to your feelings and listen to your body. Seek medical care

immediately if you have severe altitude sickness symptoms such as severe headache, nausea, or shortness of breath. Cusco has medical services that are trained to cope with altitude-related illnesses.

You can reduce the impact of altitude and make the most of your time in Cusco by taking some precautions and giving your body time to acclimate. Remember that acclimation takes time, so be patient with yourself and enjoy the one-of-a-kind experience of being in the awe-inspiring heights of the Andes.

CHAPTER FIVE

Machu Picchu: The Lost City of the Incas

Machu Picchu, the Lost City of the Incas, is a famous archaeological marvel hidden high in the Andes, amidst mist-covered peaks and lush green valleys that have captivated the minds of travelers and historians alike. Prepare to be charmed as you enter a world wrapped in mystery and wonder, where old stones murmur stories from another period.

Machu Picchu, perched on a mountaintop at an elevation of 2,430 meters (7,970 feet), is an architectural masterpiece and tribute to the Inca civilization's genius. As you approach this magnificent fortification, its magnificence gradually unfolds before your eyes. The carefully cut stone walls, perfectly aligned terraces, and beautiful craftsmanship take you to the Inca Empire's heyday.

You can't help but feel admiration for the holiness of Machu Picchu as you travel through its convoluted alleyways. With its precisely positioned windows that correspond with the solstices, the Temple of the Sun alludes at the Incas' intimate connection to the universe. The Intihuatana Stone, a mysterious carved rock, appears to have a supernatural force that has stood the test of time. And the ethereal splendor of the Temple of the Three Windows, which is embellished with delicate trapezoidal openings, will leave you in awe of the Incas' architectural genius.

But Machu Picchu is more than simply an architectural marvel; it also has significant spiritual meaning. This old citadel, surrounded by stunning natural scenery, was clearly a site of worship and reverence. The Temple of the Condor, fashioned like the majestic bird in flight, represents the Incas' close relationship with nature. And as you gaze out over the sweeping vistas from the Sun Gate or the dramatic viewpoint of Huayna Picchu, you can't help but be struck by the harmonious integration of human skill and natural power.

Beyond the sheer majesty of the ruins, Machu Picchu provides insight into Inca daily life. You can envision the Incas toiling on the mountaintop, producing their crops with steadfast determination as you visit the agricultural terraces. The Royal Residence and the Temple of the Sun provide insight into the life of the governing class, as well as its customs and ceremonies. Each stone and structure contains echoes of a thriving and complex culture that flourished millennia ago.

Consider trekking on the tough yet rewarding Inca Trail, a four-day walk through stunning landscapes, historic monuments, and various ecosystems, to properly appreciate the magic of Machu Picchu. Following in the Incas' footsteps forges a connection with the past that is as powerful as the physical journey itself.

Machu Picchu, the Lost City of the Incas, is a tribute to human creativity, spiritual connectedness, and ancient civilizations' continuing power. It beckons you to discover its mysteries, marvel at its architectural marvels, and connect with a world that has long since passed away. Prepare to be transported to a world where the old and the modern collide, where cryptic whispers from the past echo through the mist, and the spirit of the Incas lives on. Welcome to Machu Picchu's mysterious region, an encounter that will leave an unforgettable impact on your spirit.

A Tour to Machu Picchu

Machu Picchu, high in the mist-shrouded peaks of Peru's Andes, stands as a tribute to the Inca civilization's extraordinary achievements. This UNESCO World Heritage Site and one of the New Seven Wonders of the World have captured the imaginations of visitors from all over the world. Let's have a look at this incredible archaeological find.

Machu Picchu, which means "Old Mountain" in Quechua, is said to have been erected during the Inca Empire's heyday in the 15th century. It is positioned on a rocky slope overlooking the Urubamba River valley at an elevation of 2,430 meters (7,970 feet). The city remained unknown to the outside world until its rediscovery by American explorer Hiram Bingham in 1911, adding to its already captivating charm.

The site itself is around 32,500 hectares (80,000 acres) in size and contains over 150 structures, including palaces, temples, agricultural terraces, and residential complexes. The building, with finely fitted stone blocks held together without mortar, is a tribute to the Incas' excellent craftsmanship. The engineering accuracy and harmonic integration of the structures with the natural surroundings are breathtaking.

The Sacred District, located in the center of Machu Picchu, is dedicated to religious and ceremonial events. The Intihuatana Stone, a mysterious rock engraved in the shape of a sundial, is thought to have acted as an astronomical observatory and spiritual anchor. With its exquisitely sculpted masonry and interesting solar alignments, the Temple of the Sun exemplifies the Incas' great veneration for the heavenly bodies.

Aside from its architectural wonders, Machu Picchu is surrounded by a breathtaking natural landscape. The stunning backdrop of towering mountains, lush green valleys, and the meandering Urubamba River contributes to the site's mysterious ambience. For those looking for a fresh perspective on this ancient treasure, the surrounding mountains, notably the famed Huayna Picchu and Machu Picchu Mountain, provide panoramic vistas and strenuous hiking options.

Machu Picchu is a once-in-a-lifetime event that may be addressed in a variety of ways. For travelers looking for an immersive vacation, the classic Inca Trail, a multi-day hike over the Andean mountains, is a popular choice. Alternatively, you can take a picturesque train trip from Cusco to Aguas Calientes, the nearest town to Machu Picchu, followed by a bus ascent to the site, for a more accessible and less arduous approach.

Whether you visit Machu Picchu on your own or with a knowledgeable guide, the experience will leave an unforgettable mark on your soul. The tangible feeling of history, the magnificent natural surroundings, and the awe-inspiring architecture combine to create a spiritual and cultural pilgrimage that transcends time.

Exploring the Key Locations and Structures

As you enter the awe-inspiring world of Machu Picchu, you'll be surrounded by a profusion of extraordinary buildings and constructions that provide views into the Inca civilization's everyday life, spiritual beliefs, and creative creativity. Prepare to embark on an adventure as we explore some of the most important sites and structures within this historic citadel:

1. Curiosity will lead you to the Intihuatana Stone, an enigmatic engraved rock that bears witness to the Incas' strong connection to heavenly powers. This precisely positioned stone is thought to have acted as an astronomical observatory, ceremonial

center, and physical anchor connecting the spiritual and physical worlds.

2. Temple of the Sun: Marvel at the splendor of the Temple of the Sun, an architectural marvel that demonstrates the Incas' respect for the sun deity, Inti. Admire the flawlessly fitted stone walls and the exquisite trapezoidal windows that coincide with the solstices, allowing the sun's beams to infiltrate the temple in time for important celestial events.

3. Temple of the Three Windows: Be prepared to be enchanted by the Temple of the Three Windows' otherworldly splendor. This sacred site, which included three trapezoidal apertures, functioned as a place of devotion as well as a connection to the natural world. Gaze through these windows in awe, taking in the gorgeous scenery that lies beyond.

4. The Royal Residence is a series of rooms that most likely housed the Inca monarch and his retinue. Admire the exquisite stonework, carefully carved entrances, and the tranquil courtyard that formerly witnessed the Inca elite's everyday activities. Allow your imagination to take you back

in time as you imagine the majestic beauty that once adorned these chambers.

5. Temple of the Condor: Visit the Temple of the Condor to see a magnificent rock structure that mimics the outstretched wings of a flying condor. The condor is a treasured bird in Andean tradition, symbolizing power and connection to the heavens, and this location has significant spiritual importance. Consider the intricate craftsmanship and the ancient ceremonies that took place beneath these hallowed walls.

6. Agricultural Terraces: Be amazed by the incredible agricultural terraces that flow down the mountainside, a monument to the Incas' excellent engineering skills and capacity to nurture crops in difficult hilly terrain. These terraces not only served as a source of food, but also reflected the Incas' peaceful cohabitation with nature.

7. Gate of the Sun (Inti Punku): Hike to the Gate of the Sun, also known as Inti Punku, which is located at the entrance to Machu Picchu. Enjoy the amazing panoramic views of the citadel and surrounding

mountain sceneries as you pass through this stone doorway. Those who choose to embark on this journey will gain a distinct perspective and a sense of success from this vantage point.

Each site and construction of Machu Picchu tells a tale, exposing parts of the Inca civilization's amazing achievements. Allow yourself to be enveloped in the beauty, mystery, and spiritual energy that pervades this ancient citadel as you tour these principal locations. Machu Picchu is more than simply ruins; it is a living tribute to human ingenuity, reverence for environment, and the continuing heritage of a remarkable civilisation.

The Inca Trail Hike

Hiking the Inca Trail is the ultimate way to visit the beautiful citadel of Machu Picchu for explorers looking for an immersive and gratifying experience. This classic journey takes you through stunning landscapes, historic ruins, and various ecosystems before arriving at the Lost City of the Incas. Lace up your boots, embrace the spirit of exploration, and join me on this incredible journey.

The Inca Trail is a four-day trip that follows ancient stone roads, high climbs, and rough terrain for approximately 43 kilometers (26 miles). Along the trip, you'll be surrounded by the breathtaking natural beauty of the Peruvian Andes, including snow-capped mountains, dense cloud forests, and breath-taking panoramic vistas.

Day 1: Your experience begins at Kilometer 82, where you will pass through the trailhead and begin your journey. The first day consists of a moderate hike through scenic valleys and beside the raging Vilcanota River. Keep an eye out for Inca ruins along the way, such as the archaeological site of Llactapata, which gives you a taste of what's to come.

Day 2: Prepare for the most difficult, but also the most rewarding, day of the trek. Known as "Dead Woman's Pass," you'll climb to an elevation of about 4,200 meters (13,780 feet), overcoming steep inclines and tight pathways. The sense of accomplishment that comes with reaching the pass is amazing, and the panoramic vistas of the surrounding mountains make it all worthwhile.

Day 3: After a well-deserved break, Day 3 provides a variety of fascinating archaeological sites, including Runkurakay, Sayacmarca, and Phuyupatamarca. Immerse yourself in the history and mystique of these locations by learning about the Incas' architectural prowess and the significance of these structures along the pilgrimage route.

Day 4: As you make your way to Machu Picchu, the final day of the Inca Trail is the most anticipated. Arrive at the Sun Gate (Inti Punku) before dawn to see the first rays of sunshine illuminate the citadel— a truly magnificent scene. Descend inside Machu Picchu and spend the day touring the ruins, taking in the ambiance, and reflecting on the great feats of architecture and spirituality that this ancient city embodies.

Hiking the Inca Trail needs physical stamina because you'll be traveling at high altitudes for several hours each day. But the rewards are enormous: absorption in stunning natural surroundings, encounters with unique flora and fauna, and the chance to connect with the Incas' ancient past. Experienced guides will provide important insights into the culture, history, and significance of the locations you visit along the trip.

To trek the Inca Trail, you must plan ahead of time and get permits, as the number of hikers allowed on the trail is limited in order to protect its natural and cultural integrity. It is best to book your journey through a reliable tour operator that will manage logistics such as permits, camping equipment, meals, and knowledgeable guides.

Hiking the Inca Trail is a life-changing adventure that tests your physical and mental limits, rewards you with stunning scenery, and culminates in the breathtaking arrival at Machu Picchu. It's a pilgrimage that ties you to the old Inca footsteps, allowing you to form a personal bond with the past and create memories to last a lifetime. Prepare for a once-in-a-lifetime journey by following the Inca Trail to the magical treasures of Machu Picchu.

Alternative Machu Picchu Hiking Trails

While the Inca Trail is unquestionably the most famous and popular path to Machu Picchu, there are other alternate trekking trails that provide equally stunning landscape, rich history, and the opportunity to experience the Andes' grandeur. For those looking for an alternative approach to access the old fortress, these off-the-beaten-path trails offer a fresh perspective and a sense of adventure. Let's have a look at some of these incredible alternatives:

1. The Salkantay Trek is a wonderful alternative for anyone looking for magnificent alpine vistas and various landscapes. This five-day adventure takes you through snow-capped mountains, high-altitude passes, cloud forests, and even a piece of the renowned Inca Trail. The gorgeous turquoise Salkantay Lake, the majestic Salkantay Mountain, and the ability to soak in natural hot springs along the way are all highlights.

2. The Lares Trek is a remarkable tour that offers a view into Andean culture and local villages. This

four-day walk takes you through rural valleys and traditional Quechua villages, allowing you to engage with and learn about local indigenous populations. Enjoy the stunning scenery, which includes alpine lakes, craggy mountains, and bustling textile markets.

3. Choquequirao Trek: The Choquequirao Trek is an excellent choice for people wanting solitude and a sense of archaeological adventure. This strenuous six-day walk takes you to the lesser-known ancient ruins of Choquequirao, dubbed the "sister city" of Machu Picchu. Explore this hidden gem's well-preserved terraces, plazas, and temples while taking in magnificent vistas of the Apurimac River Canyon.

4. Vilcabamba Trek: The Vilcabamba Trek takes you on a historical and cultural adventure. This strenuous eight-day walk traces the last Inca resistance against the Spanish conquistadors. Explore distant archaeological sites, cross steep mountain passes, and immerse yourself in the Vilcabamba region's lush valleys and cloud forests.

5. The Inca Jungle Trek mixes trekking with exhilarating sports such as bicycling, zip-lining, and rafting for adventure seekers. This four-day adventure takes you through a variety of environments, from high mountains to tropical rainforests, with adrenaline-pumping activities along the way. After this multi-sport excursion, you'll be rejuvenated and ready to visit Machu Picchu.

Each of these alternate hiking trails offers a distinct experience, exhibiting the Andean region's natural beauty, cultural richness, and ancient wonders. There's a trail to suit your interests and sense of adventure, whether you're drawn to breathtaking mountain peaks, real cultural contacts, or the thrill of outdoor sports.

It's worth noting that, like the Inca Trail, licenses and local guides are required for these alternate routes in order to assure their preservation and sustainable tourist practices. Consider working with a reliable tour operator to handle logistics, provide expert guides, and assure your safety throughout the voyage.

Taking one of these alternate trekking pathways to Machu Picchu opens up a whole new world of exploration, allowing you to have a deeper connection with the Andean scenery and its rich history. Prepare to be astounded, challenged, and inspired as you make memories to last a lifetime, no matter which path you pick.

CHAPTER SIX

The Areas Surrounding Machu Picchu

While Machu Picchu is unquestionably the main attraction, the surrounding areas provide a plethora of natural beauty, archaeological sites, and cultural experiences that will enrich your journey. Take a minute to leave the citadel and immerse yourself in the stunning splendor that surrounds this mysterious location. Here are some of the highlights of Machu Picchu's surroundings:

1. Huayna Picchu: The distinctive peak that dominates pictures of Machu Picchu, Huayna Picchu towers above the citadel. Hike to the summit, where you'll be rewarded with stunning panoramic views of Machu Picchu and the surrounding mountain terrain. It should be noted that climbing Huayna Picchu requires a separate permit, which should be reserved in advance owing to limited availability.

2. Machu Picchu Mountain: Consider hiking Machu Picchu Mountain for an equally spectacular but slightly less crowded vista. This strenuous hike leads to the mountain's summit, which offers panoramic views of the citadel, the Urubamba River, and the neighboring peaks. This hike, like Huayna Picchu, requires a special permission.

3. Extend your trip to the stunning Sacred Valley, a place rich in ancient ruins, picturesque villages, and vibrant markets. Explore the Pisac ruins, which are noted for its outstanding agricultural terraces and beautiful stonework, as well as the Pisac Market, where you can shop for traditional products and enjoy the bustling atmosphere. Other significant Sacred Valley monuments include Ollantaytambo, Moray, and Chinchero, each of which provides distinct insights into the Inca civilisation.

4. The Maras Salt Mines are a fascinating tour into ancient salt producing technologies that have been passed down through generations. Witness the intricate network of salt terraces that cascade down the mountainside, producing an awe-inspiring

panorama. Learn about traditional salt extraction processes and the cultural relevance of this resource to local populations.

5. Explore the wonders of the Moray Archaeological Site, an interesting structure of concentric terraces resembling an amphitheater. The purpose of these terraces is unknown, while speculations claim that they could be used as an agricultural laboratory due to the different microclimates they provide. Explore the site and be amazed by Inca engineering and farming traditions.

6. Aguas Calientes: Aguas Calientes, also known as Machu Picchu Pueblo, is the gateway town to Machu Picchu and offers a dynamic ambiance with a variety of amenities for visitors. Enjoy the area's soothing hot springs, indulge in local cuisine, peruse artisan markets, or simply relax and soak up the aura of this charming mountain village.

The surrounds of Machu Picchu provide numerous possibilities to explore further into the region's natural and cultural treasures. Hiking to renowned peaks, exploring historical ruins, or immersing yourself in local communities all lends another dimension of enchantment to your adventure. If you take the time to go beyond the citadel, you'll gain a more complete grasp of the historical and environmental riches that surround Machu Picchu.

The Iconic Peak of Huayna Picchu

Huayna Picchu, which rises steeply above the historic fortress of Machu Picchu, is a beautiful monument of natural beauty and human achievement. With its steep slopes and dominating presence, this renowned peak allows intrepid guests to elevate their Machu Picchu experience to new heights—both literally and metaphorically.

Huayna Picchu, which means "Young Mountain" in Quechua, is the looming peak behind the citadel. While Machu Picchu is a sight to behold in and of itself, climbing Huayna Picchu adds an extra element of adventure and grandeur to your visit. The ascent is tough for the faint of heart, but the rewards are genuinely extraordinary.

The path to Huayna Picchu is typically dug into the mountainside and is steep and narrow. Your heart will race as you climb, not only from the physical exertion but also from the prospect of what lies ahead. The trail is peppered with stone steps, ropes for support, and stretches that border precipitous cliff, all of which add to the sense of adventure.

As you climb, you'll be rewarded with breathtaking views of Machu Picchu, the meandering Urubamba River, and the emerald peaks of the surrounding mountains. From this vantage point, the ancient castle is truly breathtaking—a huge masterpiece of Inca construction set among the beautiful Andean environment.

Reaching the summit of Huayna Picchu is an accomplishment in and of itself. You'll be rewarded with a sense of success and a beautiful vista that spreads as far as the eye can see from this tall platform. The panoramic view highlights Machu Picchu's majesty, allowing you to appreciate the citadel's magnitude and craftsmanship while simultaneously immersing you in the natural splendor that surrounds it.

Take a time at the summit to breathe in the tranquil atmosphere, marvel at the sheer vastness of the mountainscape, and ponder the ancient wonders that lay below. Standing atop Huayna Picchu provides a unique perspective, a sense of connection to the earth, and a profound admiration for the Inca civilization's creativity.

It's vital to know that access to Huayna Picchu is limited, and the walk requires a separate permit. Because of its popularity, it is best to get your permit well in advance. Furthermore, because the terrain can be tough and steep in places, it's critical to be physically and emotionally prepared for the ascent.

Huayna Picchu, with its towering presence and panoramic views, adds another degree of enchantment to Machu Picchu's already magnificent experience. It beckons adventurers, daring them to scale its heights and rewarding them with a view that few have the opportunity to see. So put on your hiking boots, enjoy the thrill of the ascent, and let Huayna Picchu take your adventure to new levels of wonder and appreciation.

A Different View of Machu Picchu Mountain

While Huayna Picchu is the most famous peak in Machu Picchu, another mountain offers a unique perspective on the ancient wonders: Machu Picchu Mountain. This spectacular peak, hidden behind the citadel, offers a distinct and awe-inspiring experience for visitors seeking a unique vantage point.

Machu Picchu Mountain, also known as Montaa Machu Picchu, is a difficult yet rewarding walk that will take you to even higher altitudes. As you climb, you'll be surrounded by rich foliage, rocky terrain, and glimpses of the spectacular ruins below. Each step leads you closer to an unrivaled view that will take your breath away in more ways than one.

In comparison to Huayna Picchu, the trek up Machu Picchu Mountain is less busy, allowing for a more calm and tranquil experience. The hike is physically challenging, with steep sections and uneven terrain, but it is well worth the effort. As you climb, you'll be rewarded with panoramic views of the citadel's majesty, the meandering Urubamba River, and the surrounding peaks.

Reaching the pinnacle of Machu Picchu Mountain is an accomplishment, and the vista that awaits you is breathtaking. From this vantage point, you'll gain a new respect for Machu Picchu's enormous size and complexity. The ancient stone monuments, terraces, and plazas show themselves in great detail, encouraging you to marvel at the Inca civilization's architectural prowess.

The surrounding mountains and valleys spread out before you, providing a picture of spectacular natural splendor. It's as if you've reached a place where time has stopped and history and nature have merged to create a scene of unsurpassed beauty. Take a time to appreciate the peace, energy, and historical significance of this wonderful location.

As with any hiking adventure, it's critical to be prepared. Make sure you have good boots, enough drink, and a modest level of fitness to undertake the difficult ascent. Permits are required to trek Machu Picchu Mountain, and they should be obtained ahead of time to ensure your place on this incredible journey.

Hiking Machu Picchu Mountain allows you to see the citadel from a different angle, obtain a better appreciation of its architectural wonders, and interact with the natural beauty that surrounds it. It's a chance to get away from the masses, discover serenity in the mountains, and see the magic of Machu Picchu emerge before your eyes.

Set your eyes on Machu Picchu Mountain if you're looking for a fresh perspective, a quieter trip, and an encounter that blends physical exertion with exceptional rewards.

Investigating the Sun Gate (Inti Punku)

The Sun Gate, or Inti Punku in Quechua, is perched high above the citadel of Machu Picchu, beckoning adventurers seeking a unique perspective on this ancient wonder. Following in the footsteps of the ancient Incas, reaching the Sun Gate reveals a spectacular vista that has captivated the imaginations of travelers for generations.

The Sun Gate is a figurative entry into a world cloaked in mystery and enchantment, not just a physical portal. It was thought to be a ceremonial entry to Machu Picchu, where the rising sun would cast golden rays on the citadel during the winter solstice, signaling an auspicious occasion in the Inca calendar.

The famed Inca Trail serves as the starting point for the journey to the Sun Gate. The anticipation grows with each step as you cross the old stone pathways, surrounded by pure environment and awe-inspiring scenery. The walk winds through cloud forests, old ruins, and gently sloping hills, immersing you in the atmosphere of the Andes.

The air is filled with excitement and devotion as you approach the Sun Gate. The final ascent needs a final burst of energy, but the pleasure at the top is indescribable. As you pass through the stone gate, a breathtaking view opens in front of you—Machu Picchu lays below, seemingly undisturbed by time, enveloped by the craggy mountains and framed by the great expanse of the Urubamba River valley.

From this vantage point, you can see the vast grandeur and exquisite planning that went into building Machu Picchu. The terraces, temples, and stone constructions merge in with the natural contours of the environment, providing an awe-inspiring and humbling image. Take a minute to soak in the magical ambiance, contemplate on the Inca civilization's genius, and marvel at the incredible beauty that surrounds you.

The Sun Gate affords not only an amazing view of Machu Picchu, but also a unique viewpoint on the journey itself. Standing at this point, you can reflect on the trials you overcame, the physical and mental strength required to get here, and your spiritual connection to the hallowed land of the Incas.

To see the Sun Gate, one must hike the legendary Inca Trail. Permits are required, and owing to limited availability, it is critical to plan and book well in advance. It's also a good idea to hire an experienced guide who can explain the history, culture, and significance of the locations along the way.

The Sun Gate is a tribute to Machu Picchu's eternal fascination and the spirit of adventure. It invites you to transcend the commonplace and embrace the remarkable. Prepare to have your breath taken away and your sense of wonder kindled as you pass through this ancient doorway. The Sun Gate is a portal to adventure, self-discovery, and the everlasting mysteries that lay within Machu Picchu's heart.

Aguas Calientes, Ollantaytambo, and Other Nearby Attractions

While Machu Picchu takes center stage, there are other neighboring attractions that should be on your agenda. From the lovely hamlet of Aguas Calientes to the ancient ruins of Ollantaytambo, these locations provide insight into the region's rich cultural and historical legacy. Here are some must-see attractions around Machu Picchu:

1. Aguas Calientes (Machu Picchu Pueblo): Aguas Calientes is the entryway to Machu Picchu, located at the foot of the mountains. Despite its tiny size, the town has a lively ambiance, with bustling markets, cobblestone streets, and a delectable assortment of restaurants serving both local and foreign food. After a day of exploring, relax in the soothing thermal baths or browse the artisan markets for one-of-a-kind gifts.

2. Ollantaytambo: Ollantaytambo, located in the Sacred Valley of the Incas, is a living witness of Inca engineering and design. The spectacular stone

terraces, temples, and ceremonial sites are among the well-preserved ruins. Explore the ancient fortification, climb Temple Hill for panoramic views, and learn about the strategic importance of this Inca stronghold.

3. Pisac: Known for its bustling market and awe-inspiring ruins, Pisac provides an enthralling mix of cultural activities. Explore the lively market, where sellers sell handicrafts, fabrics, and traditional products. Visit the archaeological site, which is set on a hilltop, and marvel at the elaborate agricultural terraces and well-preserved structures that offer a window into Inca history.

4. Discover the mystery of Moray, an ancient site famous for its strange circular terraces. The Incas used these terraces, which resembled an amphitheater, as a unique experimental agricultural laboratory. Explore the site, marvel at the perfection of the terraces, and reflect on the ancient engineering and scientific understanding that contributed to the Inca civilization's thriving.

5. Maras Salt Mines: Visit the Maras Salt Mines to learn about the fascinating world of salt manufacture. These salt terraces have been used since pre-Inca times and are still harvested by local communities today. Witness the enthralling patterns generated by salty water evaporation and learn about the traditional procedures passed down through centuries. The breathtaking scenery provides numerous photo opportunities.

6. Chinchero: Visit Chinchero, a lovely community famed for its textile traditions, to immerse yourself in traditional Andean culture. Investigate the local market for elaborately woven textiles and vivid handicrafts. Visit the colonial chapel built on the ruins of an Inca palace and watch a traditional weaving demonstration to learn about the ancient skills that are still used today.

Each of these neighboring attractions provides a distinct view of the region's rich history and cultural heritage. Whether you're visiting Aguas Calientes' cobblestone alleyways, climbing ancient ruins in Ollantaytambo, or discovering the captivating traditions of Chinchero, these sites enhance your Machu Picchu tour by providing depth and variety to your overall experience.

Take the time to see these neighboring attractions, and you'll be rewarded with a better appreciation of the Andean civilization and its lasting impact. Each location has its own tale to tell, and when combined, they create a tapestry of captivating experiences that will leave an everlasting impact on your journey through this extraordinary part of the world.

CHAPTER SEVEN

Practical Advice and Suggestions

1. Organize and Book Early: Because Machu Picchu is a popular tourist site, it's critical to organize your trip ahead of time. Obtain permits for Machu Picchu, Huayna Picchu, Machu Picchu Mountain, and any other attractions that require them. Also, reserve your lodging and transportation early to ensure availability.

2. Adapt to the Altitude: Because Machu Picchu is located at a high elevation, it is critical to adapt before engaging in any physical activities. Spend a few days in Cusco or other high-altitude places to gradually acclimate your body. Stay hydrated, avoid strenuous physical activity at first, and consult a healthcare expert if you have any concerns.

3. Layer your clothing: The weather in the region may be unpredictable, with temperature swings throughout the day. Dress in layers to accommodate temperature variations, and bring a

111

rain jacket or poncho in case of rain. Exploring the ruins and hiking trails requires comfortable walking shoes with good traction.

4. Stay Hydrated and Pack Snacks: At high elevations, hydration is critical, so bring a refillable water bottle and drink enough of fluids throughout your adventure. Pack some light snacks, such as energy bars, bananas, or almonds, to keep you fueled during your adventures.

5. Protect yourself from the Sun: Because the sun can be harsh at high altitudes, wear a wide-brimmed hat, sunglasses, and sunscreen with a high SPF. Carry a little travel-sized sunscreen with you for reapplication throughout the day.

6. Consider Hiring a professional Guide: Hire a professional guide who can provide insight into the history, culture, and significance of Machu Picchu and its surrounds. A guide can enhance your experience by offering fascinating anecdotes, answering questions, and assisting you in more effectively navigating the sites.

7. Respect the Sacred Sites: Machu Picchu is a UNESCO World Heritage site with significant cultural and historical importance. Respect the site's norms and regulations, such as not touching or climbing on the remains, not littering, and following designated walkways. Be environmentally conscious and leave no evidence of your visit.

8. Capture the Moment: Bring a good camera or smart phone to capture Machu Picchu's beauty and grandeur. Remember to bring spare memory cards and batteries. Take your time to locate unusual angles and perspectives, but don't forget to put the camera down every now and then to immerse yourself in the present moment.

9. Be Aware of Altitude Sickness: Different people react differently to altitude sickness. Take it easy if you have symptoms like a headache, dizziness, nausea, or shortness of breath, and seek medical attention if necessary. Mild symptoms might be relieved with Coca tea or candies.

10. Immerse yourself in the Experience: Finally, remember to slow down, take deep breaths, and

genuinely absorb Machu Picchu's beauty and significance. Allow you to be fully present in the moment and absorb the enchantment of this unique location. Listen to the wind's stories, sense the ancient spirit, and allow the wonder of Machu Picchu to leave an unforgettable stamp on your soul.

You'll be well-prepared to embark on a fascinating and enriching journey to Machu Picchu if you follow these practical suggestions and recommendations. Accept the challenge, accept the history, and let the ancient wonders of this hallowed site to captivate your heart and mind.

Best Photography Locations

Machu Picchu, with its beautiful natural surroundings and awe-inspiring architecture, provides photographers with numerous opportunities to create stunning photographs. Here are some of the best photographic places at Machu

Picchu, ranging from prominent perspectives to secret corners:

1. Head to the Guardhouse (also known as the Caretaker's Hut) for that iconic postcard image of Machu Picchu. This vantage point provides a spectacular view of the entire citadel, with the famed Huayna Picchu in the distance.

2. The Intihuatana Stone, an artistically carved stone pillar, is not only an important archaeological feature but also a superb photographic subject. Its location near the Temple of the Sun affords a one-of-a-kind opportunity to experience the essence of old Inca artistry.

3. Sun Gate (Inti Punku): Follow the Inca Trail to the Sun Gate for a bird's-eye perspective of Machu Picchu. The view from here is just stunning, with the ancient ruins framed by the surrounding mountains. It's an excellent location for capturing the citadel's grandeur and magnitude.

4. Explore the Inca Bridge, a stone roadway that formerly served as a gateway to Machu Picchu. This

hidden gem provides a unique perspective and an opportunity to photograph architectural marvels against the beautiful green landscape.

5. The Temple of the Condor is an intriguing location that demonstrates the brilliance of Inca stonework. This location has rock formations that look like a condor with its wings spread. To capture the subtle intricacies of this sacred location, experiment with different perspectives and compositions.

6. Terrace Views: Machu Picchu is famous for its spectacular terraces, which were precisely built to improve agricultural efficiency. The terraces provide not only breathtaking views, but also an opportunity to depict the Inca civilization's symmetrical beauty and architectural accuracy.

7. If you're looking for a difficult journey, consider climbing Huayna Picchu, the famed peak that overlooks Machu Picchu. You'll be rewarded with a stunning view of the citadel tucked among the mountains from the summit, providing for an unforgettable shooting experience.

Visit the Inti Watana stone, an ancient sundial used by the Incas to track the sun's journey. This one-of-a-kind feature, paired with the surrounding scenery, provides a mysterious atmosphere that can be brilliantly portrayed through photography.

8. Putucusi Mountain: For a less-known destination, consider climbing up Putucusi Mountain, which is located opposite Machu Picchu. You'll get a new viewpoint of the citadel from its pinnacle, with spectacular views of the Urubamba River and the surrounding verdant woodlands.

9. Sunrise and Sunset: Seeing the sunrise or sunset at Machu Picchu is a once-in-a-lifetime experience. Capture the warm golden light that illuminates the ancient stone structures as the sun rises or when the sun sets behind the mountains. These airy and intriguing image opportunities are created by these moments.

While taking great photographs is enjoyable, it is critical to follow the rules and restrictions in place to conserve Machu Picchu. Follow the established walkways, avoid climbing on the ruins, and be respectful of other visitors. Allow yourself to be immersed in the wonder of the site, and allow your images to represent the beauty and historical value of this magnificent location.

Hiring a Guide or Going It Alone

One essential option to make when arranging a trip to Machu Picchu is whether to hire a guide or explore the site on your own. Both alternatives have advantages, and the decision ultimately comes down to your tastes, money, and level of comfort. Here are some things to think about when selecting whether to hire a guide or go it alone:

1. Hiring a professional guide can enhance your experience by delivering in-depth historical and cultural insights. They can tell you fascinating anecdotes about the Inca civilization, explain the significance of various constructions, and help you grasp Machu Picchu's intricate history. A guide can bring the place to life by explaining its significance and the mysteries that surround it.

2. Machu Picchu is a large complex with many structures, terraces, and routes to navigate. Without sufficient instruction, navigating the site can be intimidating. A guide can assist you in smoothly navigating the site, ensuring you don't miss any vital aspects and make the most of your time there. They can guide you to hidden nooks and vistas that you might not have discovered otherwise.

3. While Machu Picchu is generally safe to explore, having a guide at your side can provide an added sense of protection, especially if you're inexperienced with the area or worried about potential risks. A guide can advise you on safety precautions, keep you aware of any applicable precautions, and aid you in the event of any unanticipated occurrences.

4. Flexibility and Independence: Exploring Machu Picchu on your own gives you more flexibility and independence. You can go at your own speed, spend more time at the locations that are most interesting to you, and take breaks anytime you choose. You are free to explore the citadel at your

leisure, providing for a more intimate and introspective experience.

5. Budget Factors: Hiring a guide incurs an additional expense, which may influence your selection. Consider your budget and whether the value supplied by a guide is worth the cost. Exploring Machu Picchu on your own can be a more cost-effective choice if you're on a tight budget.

6. Prior Knowledge and Research: If you've done significant research on Machu Picchu and are confident in your comprehension of its history and significance, you may be able to explore independently. If, on the other hand, you want to expand your knowledge and learn new perspectives, a guide can provide essential insights that go beyond what you can find in guidebooks or online resources.

Whether you hire a guide or go it alone is a matter of personal decision and the type of experience you seek. A guide can substantially enhance your experience if you are interested in history, culture, and acquiring a complete understanding of Machu

Picchu. Going solo, on the other hand, may be the best option if you like the flexibility to explore at your own speed and plunge into a more introspective experience.

Whatever decision you choose, remember to follow the rules and regulations in place to protect the site. Take the time to immerse yourself in the awe-inspiring beauty of Machu Picchu, comprehend its historical significance, and create lasting memories of this extraordinary site, whether you're escorted by a tour or exploring yourself.

Tourism Safety and Responsibility

It is critical to consider safety and responsible tourism when visiting Machu Picchu. You can help preserve this ancient wonder for future generations by being careful of your activities and respecting the environment. Here are some crucial safety and responsible tourist reminders:

1. Follow the Guidelines and restrictions: To protect the site and for the safety of visitors, Machu Picchu

has guidelines and restrictions in place. Acquaint yourself with these guidelines and follow them during your visit. This includes refraining from touching or climbing on the remains, adhering to defined walkways, and respecting any restricted areas.

2. Stay Hydrated and Prepare for Altitude: Machu Picchu is located at a high altitude, so staying hydrated is essential to avoiding altitude sickness. Drink plenty of water during your vacation and consider bringing a refillable water bottle with you. Additionally, spend a few days acclimating to the altitude in Cusco or other high-altitude places before visiting Machu Picchu.

3. Keep Your Physical Fitness in Mind: Exploring Machu Picchu entails trekking and navigating difficult terrain. Determine your degree of physical fitness and select activities and hikes that are appropriate for your skills. To avoid exhaustion or injury, pace yourself, take breaks as needed, and listen to your body.

4. Pack carefully: It is critical to pack carefully when visiting Machu Picchu. Bring reusable water bottles, snacks in reusable containers, and toiletries that are eco-friendly. Avoid single-use plastics and dispose of trash in designated bins to reduce waste.

5. Respect the Site's Sacredness: Machu Picchu is rich in cultural and historical significance. Respect the ruins by not climbing on or touching them, as this can cause harm. Respect any prohibited locations or ceremonies and follow the advice of local guides. This ensures that the site's integrity is preserved.

6. Support Local Communities: Practice responsible tourism by donating to local charities and businesses. Choose hotels, restaurants, and tour operators who prioritize sustainability and assist the local economy. Purchase locally manufactured souvenirs and crafts to support the villages surrounding Machu Picchu.

7. Leave No Trace: The natural beauty of Machu Picchu is a treasure that must be conserved. Leave no sign of your presence by not littering or leaving

any rubbish behind. Respect the environment and leave Machu Picchu as you left it so that future visitors might marvel at its splendor.

8. Listen to Guides and Authorities: Pay attention to the advice of authorized staff, such as guides and park rangers. They are well-versed in the history of the site, as well as its safety standards and environmental conservation activities. Following their recommendations makes everyone's experience safer and more enjoyable.

9. Be Mindful of Photography: While photographing memories is fantastic, be courteous of others and avoid disrupting the experience of other guests. Respect the privacy of people, follow any photography guidelines, and never use flash photography on sensitive objects or structures.

10. Educate Yourself: Before traveling to Machu Picchu, learn about its history, culture, and significance. Understanding the context of this ancient treasure will increase your admiration and allow you to interact with it more properly.

You can help to preserve Machu Picchu for the long future by prioritizing safety and practicing responsible tourism. Enjoy the awe, immerse yourself in its rich history, and leave a great impression by being a respectful and conscientious guest.

Cultural Etiquette and Site Respect

It is critical to observe cultural etiquette and respect for the place when visiting Machu Picchu. Machu Picchu is both an archaeological marvel and a spiritual site with significant cultural importance. You can honor the history and customs associated with this ancient monument by following basic etiquette requirements. Here are some important cultural etiquette guidelines to remember:

1. Dress politely: It is advised to dress modestly and politely when visiting Machu Picchu. Cover your shoulders, prevent exposed apparel, and dress comfortably for the weather circumstances. You demonstrate respect for the cultural significance of

the site and the local customs by wearing appropriately.

2. Follow Photography Guidelines: Photography is a great way to remember your visit, but it's vital to be respectful when taking images. Follow any photography guidelines issued by authorities or tour guides. Be considerate to other guests and avoid invading their privacy or interfering with their experience.

3. Speak Softly and Avoid Disruptive Behavior: Machu Picchu is a serene and spiritually significant location. Maintain a low voice and avoid loud conversations or disruptive behavior that could break the peaceful atmosphere. By speaking softly, you allow others to experience the natural beauty of the location as well as connect with its historical aura.

4. Respect Sacred areas: Machu Picchu contains sacred areas and ceremonial locations of immense spiritual significance. Respect these locations by not touching or climbing on them. Obey the instructions

of authorized staff and any restrictions or rituals associated with certain venues.

5. Avoid littering and protect the environment: The pristine environment of Machu Picchu is a vital component of its allure. Please help to preserve its natural beauty by not littering or leaving any rubbish behind. Place rubbish in designated containers and encourage others to do the same. You help to preserve the place for future generations by leaving it clean.

6. Learn and Appreciate the History: Before your visit, educate yourself about the history and significance of Machu Picchu. Understanding the site's cultural and historical context will allow you to understand its importance and connect more closely with its tale. Engage with local guides or educational materials to obtain a thorough knowledge.

7. Participate in Responsible Tourism: Responsible tourism is critical to preserving Machu Picchu's integrity. Support local towns and companies, select environmentally friendly lodgings and tour operators, and be conscious of your environmental

impact. Responsible tourism contributes to the long-term viability of the place as well as the well-being of the local people.

8. Observe and Follow Local Customs: Machu Picchu is situated within the greater cultural setting of Peru. Learn the fundamental Peruvian customs and traditions, such as greetings and expressions of thanks. Respecting local norms promotes cultural understanding and improves your entire experience.

Remember that Machu Picchu is more than just a tourist destination; it has enormous historical, cultural, and spiritual value. By practicing cultural etiquette and showing respect for the site and its surrounds, you honor the heritage of this magnificent location while also making the experience more meaningful and memorable for yourself and others.

CHAPTER EIGHT

After Machu Picchu

While Machu Picchu is unquestionably the highlight of any trip to Peru, the country also has a plethora of other wonderful attractions that should not be overlooked. Peru has something for everyone, from vibrant cities to natural treasures. Here are some ideas for visiting the various beauties that lie beyond Machu Picchu:

1. Lima: Begin your tour in Lima's vibrant capital city. Discover Lima's historic center, a UNESCO World Heritage site with wonderfully maintained colonial buildings. Indulge in Peruvian cuisine that combines indigenous, European, and Asian flavors. Visit the Larco Museum, which holds a large collection of pre-Columbian art and artifacts.

2. Cusco: While Machu Picchu is the region's main draw, Cusco is nevertheless a fascinating city worth exploring. Explore its cobblestone lanes, which are bordered with Inca walls and colonial buildings.

Explore the colorful San Pedro Market, a sensory feast of colors, smells, and fragrances, and the awe-inspiring Qorikancha, once the most significant Inca temple. Cusco is also an excellent starting point for seeing the Sacred Valley and other adjacent archaeological sites.

3. Arequipa: Known as the "White City" because of its spectacular colonial architecture made of white volcanic stone, Arequipa is a charming southern Peruvian resort. Discover the Santa Catalina Monastery, a lovely collection of colorful buildings and peaceful grounds. Admire the majestic Misti Volcano, which serves as a dramatic backdrop to the city. Arequipa is also the starting point for trips to the Colca Canyon, one of the world's deepest canyons and a haven for spectacular Andean condors.

4. Lake Titicaca: Visit Lake Titicaca, the world's highest navigable lake, for a high-altitude wonder. Take a boat excursion to the Uros Islands, which are entirely made of reeds and where you can learn about the Uros people's traditional way of life.

Explore Taquile Island, which is famed for its delicate textile workmanship and gorgeous lake views. The tranquil splendor of Lake Titicaca and its surrounding scenery will astound you.

5. Discover the enigma of the Nazca Lines, which are massive geoglyphs etched into the desert floor. Fly over the lines for a beautiful journey to properly admire their detailed designs, which include animals, vegetation, and geometric shapes. The Nazca Lines are a witness to the ancient civilisation that once flourished in the region, and they continue to pique the interest of experts and visitors alike.

6. Amazon Rainforest: Immerse yourself in the Amazon Rainforest's astounding richness. Explore lush habitats, spot exotic creatures, and learn about indigenous cultures' traditional ways of life on a jungle expedition. You can take guided trips or river cruises from Iquitos or Puerto Maldonado, which provide unforgettable experiences in this natural wonderland.

These are just a few of the many great places to visit in Peru besides Machu Picchu. Each region has its own distinct set of attractions, ranging from archaeological marvels to natural vistas and cultural experiences. Peru has plenty to offer every traveler, whether they are looking for history, adventure, nature, or gastronomy, ensuring a truly remarkable journey.

The Sacred Valley Exploration

The Sacred Valley of Peru, nestled within the majestic Andes Mountains, is a mesmerizing place with significant historical, cultural, and environmental value. The Sacred Valley, with its lush scenery, historic ruins, and active local villages, provides a plethora of experiences for travelers looking to immerse themselves in Peru's rich legacy. Here are some highlights and must-see sights in this wonderful location to explore:

1. Pisac: Begin your tour at Pisac, which is noted for its magnificent Inca ruins and thriving artisan

market. Explore the Pisac Archaeological Park's terraces and spectacular stone buildings, which provide sweeping views of the valley. Explore the market for complex handicrafts, bright textiles, and one-of-a-kind souvenirs made by local craftsmen.

2. Ollantaytambo: Travel farther into the Sacred Valley to the old Inca settlement of Ollantaytambo. This well-preserved ancient site features magnificent stone terraces, intricate water canals, and the massive Temple of the Sun. Climb to the top of the ruins for panoramic views of the surrounding mountains and insight into the Incas' strategic planning.

3. Moray: Explore Moray's agricultural miracle, a system of circular terraces that served as an experimental agricultural laboratory for the Incas. Admire the accuracy of these concentric terraces, which produced microclimates for cultivating a variety of crops. Moray's unusual design and engineering make it an intriguing archaeological site to examine.

4. Discover the stunning salt mines of Maras, just a short distance from Moray. Thousands of salt pans tumbling down the mountainside make up this old salt producing complex. Take a walk around the pools and see how the villagers are carrying on a centuries-old tradition of salt extraction. The vivid white salt pans against the Sacred Valley backdrop provide a wonderfully stunning view.

5. Chinchero: Immerse yourself in traditional Andean culture by visiting Chinchero. Discover the colonial chapel constructed on Inca ruins and the delicate craft of cloth weaving. Traditional weaving skills are demonstrated by local women, and beautifully woven textiles represent the region's rich textile legacy.

6. Andean settlements: Visit indigenous settlements in the Sacred Valley to immerse yourself in local culture. Engage with the locals to learn about their culture and their way of life. To enhance your connection to Andean traditions, engage in community-based tourist activities such as farming, pottery-making, or traditional culinary lessons.

7. Scenic Landscapes: The Sacred Valley is known for its breathtaking natural beauty, which complements its cultural attractions. Enjoy breathtaking vistas of towering mountains, verdant valleys, and winding rivers. Hike or ride your bike across the stunning landscapes to truly experience the region's natural beauties.

Keep in mind the importance of responsible tourism as you explore the Sacred Valley. Respect the local community, adhere to all guidelines and regulations, and leave no sign of your stay. Supporting local businesses and purchasing locally created items helps to ensure the region's long-term growth.

The Sacred Valley of Peru invites you to travel back in time and see the wonders of ancient civilizations, vivid customs, and stunning landscapes. From ancient sites to cultural experiences, this amazing region will awe you and leave you with lasting memories of your Peruvian adventure.

Vinicunca (Rainbow Mountain)

The Rainbow Mountain, also known as Vinicunca or Montaa de Siete Colores, is perched high in Peru's Andes Mountains and has swiftly become one of the country's most popular natural attractions. With its dazzling display of vivid colors and stunning sceneries, this awe-inspiring geological wonder has caught the hearts of travelers. Here's all you need to know about visiting Rainbow Mountain:

1. Location and Access: The Rainbow Mountain is located in the Cusco region, not far from Cusco proper. However, getting to this natural wonder takes some work and perseverance. A multi-hour drive from Cusco is usually followed by a strenuous walk to an elevation of over 5,000 meters (16,400 feet) above sea level. Because of the high altitude and strenuous conditions, it is critical to fully acclimate and be prepared for the physical demands of the walk.

2. Natural Color Phenomenon: What distinguishes Rainbow Mountain is its beautiful spectrum of colors that spans the mountainside. These hues are

caused by mineral deposits such as iron oxide, copper, and sulfur that have oxidized over millions of years, resulting in vivid bands of red, pink, yellow, and green. The hues increase as the sun illuminates the mountain, creating a genuinely captivating scene that is often compared to a painter's masterpiece.

3. Hiking Experience: The hike to Rainbow Mountain is a difficult experience, but the benefits are well worth it. Depending on your fitness level and acclimatization, the hike could last several hours. You'll be treated to beautiful vistas of the surrounding Andean scenery as you pass through valleys, cross rivers, and meet the indigenous inhabitants that call this region home. To guarantee a comfortable and pleasurable hike, take suitable clothing, water, snacks, and sunscreen.

4. Beyond the natural grandeur, the Rainbow Mountain walk provides an opportunity to meet with local populations, such as the Quechua people, who have lived in this region for millennia. Locals dressed in traditional garb may be encountered

along the trail, herding llamas and alpacas or giving refreshments to hikers. Engage with the locals to learn about their way of life and their rich cultural heritage.

5. Responsible Tourism: As the Rainbow Mountain's popularity has grown, it is critical to prioritize responsible tourism. Respect the environment by staying on authorized trails, appropriately disposing of rubbish, and avoiding any harm to the sensitive ecosystem. Support local communities by hiring local guides and buying souvenirs directly from craftspeople.

The Rainbow Mountain provides a once-in-a-lifetime opportunity to observe nature's splendor in all its brilliant glory. You'll be overcome with surprise and awe as you stand at the summit, surrounded by a kaleidoscope of hues. This natural wonder epitomizes Peru's great diversity and magnificence, providing another layer of enchantment to your tour through this remarkable country.

Excursions to the Amazon Rainforest

The Amazon Rainforest is a fascinating and biodiversity habitat that spans numerous South American countries, including Peru. An Amazon rainforest expedition allows you to explore the heart of nature's green paradise, where you may see an astounding variety of species, lush flora, and ancient indigenous civilizations. Here's what you need to know to make the most of your trip to the Amazon rainforest:

1. When organizing your Amazon jungle vacation, you'll need to choose a base from which to explore the surrounding area. Iquitos and Puerto Maldonado are two popular destinations in Peru. Iquitos is in the northern Peruvian Amazon and may be reached by boat or aircraft, but Puerto Maldonado is in the southern Amazon and can be reached by a short flight from Cusco or Lima. Both destinations provide unique experiences, so think about your tastes and interests before making a decision.

2. Exploring the Amazon Rainforest: After arriving at your base, you'll go on guided excursions into the Amazon rainforest. These can include jungle walks, river boat excursions, and even nighttime trips to see the forest's nocturnal residents. Guides will walk you through the dense forest, showing you intriguing species like as monkeys, colorful birds, sloths, and possibly even elusive jaguars. You'll have the opportunity to learn about the intricate ecosystem as well as the therapeutic plants on which indigenous populations have relied for ages.

3. Canopy Walkways and Towers: If you want to completely immerse yourself in the jungle, visit the canopy walkways and towers. These towering platforms offer an uncommon view of the forest, allowing you to walk among the treetops and see the fascinating interplay of plant and fauna. From here, you can see colourful birds, monkeys swinging through the trees, and maybe even a sloth gliding gently in slow motion.

4. River Cruises: Exploring the Amazon would be incomplete without a trip down its twisting rivers.

River cruises provide a tranquil and scenic way to see the splendor of the rainforest while gliding along the calm rivers. Keep a watch out for pink river dolphins, caimans, enormous river otters, and a variety of bird species on these trips. You may also have the opportunity to visit local riverfront communities and learn about their traditional way of life.

5. Indigenous Communities & Cultural Experiences: Engaging with indigenous communities and learning about their unique cultures and traditions is a highlight of visiting the Amazon Rainforest. Many excursions include trips to local communities, where you can engage with locals, see traditional ceremonies, sample traditional cuisine, and even take part in craft-making activities. These experiences provide a better understanding of the indigenous people's tight affinity with the natural world.

6. Responsible Tourism: It is critical to prioritize responsible and sustainable tourism when visiting the Amazon. Choose trustworthy tour companies

who stress environmental conservation and community support. Respect the forest and its people by adhering to the instructions of your guides, abstaining from littering, and avoiding any activity that may affect the fragile environment.

A trip to the Amazon rainforest is a life-changing event that will leave you in awe of the natural world's beauty and intricacy. This voyage will increase your awareness for the Earth's most diversified ecosystem, from colorful wildlife encounters to cultural immersion. Prepare to be amazed by the Amazon's sights, sounds, and scents as you make lifelong memories in this lush green paradise.

CHAPTER NINE

FAQ (Frequently Asked Questions)

1. Q: Is it worthwhile to visit Machu Picchu?

A: Without a doubt! Machu Picchu is a World Heritage Site recognized by UNESCO and one of the New Seven Wonders of the World. Its stunning beauty, historical significance, and beautiful location in the Andes make it a must-see destination for visitors.

2. Q: How long does the Inca Trail take to hike?

A: The conventional Inca Trail journey typically lasts four days and three nights. This entails hiking around 43 kilometers (26 miles) and reaching the Sun Gate on the final day to access Machu Picchu. There are, however, shorter trekking options, such as the two-day Inca Trail or alternate treks such as the Salkantay Trek.

3. Q: Do I need to buy tickets ahead of time to visit Machu Picchu?

A: Yes, booking your Machu Picchu tickets in advance is strongly advised, especially during peak tourist season. The number of visitors per day is limited, and tickets frequently sell out. Tickets can be purchased online or through authorized travel companies.

4. Q: Is there a risk of altitude sickness when visiting Machu Picchu?

A: Because of its great elevation, altitude sickness can be a worry when visiting Machu Picchu. It is critical to adequately acclimate before engaging in any physical activities and to stay hydrated. Slowing down and allowing your body to acclimate to the altitude will reduce your chances of altitude sickness.

5. Q: When is the ideal time to go to Machu Picchu?

A: The dry season, which runs from May to September, is widely regarded as the finest time to visit Machu Picchu. Typically, the weather is more consistent, with fewer rain showers. However, keep in mind that these months also draw a greater number of tourists. The rainy season, which runs from October to April, receives more rain but is still a fantastic time to come because the scenery are lush and the crowds are lower.

6. A: Do I need a visa to travel to Peru?

A: Visa requirements for Peru differ according on nationality. Many nations, including the United States, Canada, the United Kingdom, Australia, and the majority of European Union countries, do not require a visa for tourism stays of up to 90 days. However, it is always advisable to check the most recent visa requirements for your place of residency before visiting.

7. Q: Can I visit Machu Picchu in a single day?

A: It is feasible to visit Machu Picchu on a day trip, but careful planning is required. The majority of day journeys include boarding an early morning train from Cusco or Ollantaytambo to Aguas Calientes, the town at Machu Picchu's base. You can then take a bus or hike to the archaeological site. Keep in mind that visiting Machu Picchu in a single day means having limited time at the monument, so consider staying overnight for a more immersive experience.

8. Q: Are there places to stay near Machu Picchu?

A: Yes, there are hotels in Aguas Calientes, the village at the foot of Machu Picchu. There are a variety of hotels, hostels, and lodges to suit all budgets. Staying in Aguas Calientes overnight allows you to visit Machu Picchu at different times of the day and experience the tranquil ambiance before the mass of day visitors arrive.

9. Q: Is it possible to see Machu Picchu without hiking?

A: Yes, it is possible to see Machu Picchu without hiking. Alternative transportation choices include riding a bus or hiring a shuttle from Aguas Calientes to the Machu Picchu entrance. Keep in mind, though, that there is still some walking involved within the archaeological site itself, as it is quite large.

When is it best to visit Machu Picchu

The dry season, which lasts from May to September, is the finest time to explore Machu Picchu. During this time, expect brighter skies, little rain, and generally pleasant weather. The months of June, July, and August are especially popular, although they can sometimes be crowded.

Visiting during the dry season provides improved vision and allows you to fully enjoy the magnificent landscapes that surround Machu Picchu. You'll also have a better chance of getting stunning images without the impediment of rain or fog.

However, keep in mind that the dry season is also peak tourist season, so expect greater crowds and higher expenses for lodging and transportation. To secure your desired dates, purchase your tickets and lodgings well in advance.

If you wish to avoid crowds and have a more peaceful experience, visit Machu Picchu during the shoulder seasons, which are April to May and September to October. The weather can still be pleasant throughout these months, with fewer visitors than during the peak season.

The rainy season lasts from November to March in Machu Picchu, with February being the wettest month. While rain can create a mystical mood at the location, it can also reduce visibility and make trekking trails more difficult. Visiting during the rainy season, on the other hand, have perks such as beautiful green sceneries and fewer tourists.

The optimum time to visit Machu Picchu is determined by your individual choices and priorities. Consider weather, crowd levels, and your ideal travel experience when deciding on the best time to travel.

How can I receive Inca Trail permits

Obtaining Inca Trail permits is an important step in arranging your trip to Machu Picchu. The following are the main measures to take:

1. Choose a trustworthy travel operator: The first step is to find a trustworthy tour company that offers Inca Trail packages. Booking your journey with a licensed operator is essential since they will handle the permit application procedure on your behalf.

2. Plan ahead of time: Inca Trail permits are limited and sell out quickly, particularly during peak season (May to September). To ensure your favorite dates, it is best to schedule your expedition at least six months in advance.

3. Confirm availability: Before finishing your booking, make sure that your preferred tour operator has permits available for the days you want to trek. They will be able to supply you with the most recent permit availability information.

4. Once you've decided on a tour operator, you'll need to submit them with your personal information, such as your complete name, passport number, country, and date of birth. The permission application requires this information.

5. Make a deposit/payment: To secure your booking, most tour operators will want a deposit or full payment. Payment methods vary, so check with your operator to see what they prefer.

6. Permit application: The permit application process will be handled on your behalf by your tour operator. They will gather the essential information from you and submit your application to the authorities in charge of the Inca Trail.

7. Confirmation of permits: After completing the permit application, your tour operator will tell you when the permits are confirmed. They will give you with all of the relevant papers and information about your adventure.

8. Check your permit details: Once you obtain your permit, double-check that all of the information,

including your name, passport number, and trek dates, is correct. Any disagreements should be resolved with your tour provider.

It's vital to remember that Inca Trail permits are non-transferable and non-refundable, so be sure you've finalized your trip plans before applying for permits.

You can get your Inca Trail permits and start on an incredible journey to Machu Picchu by following these procedures and dealing with a trustworthy tour operator.

Are there any Rules or Requirements to Follow When Visiting Machu Picchu

Yes, there are various limits and rules in place when visiting Machu Picchu in order to protect the site and guarantee that all visitors have a safe and sustainable experience. Here are a few crucial rules to bear in mind:

1. Entrance tickets: To enter Machu Picchu, all visitors must have a valid entrance ticket, which may be purchased in advance online or through approved ticketing companies. Tickets are limited and should be purchased in advance, especially during peak season.

2. Timed entry slots: To regulate visitor flow, Machu Picchu admission is segregated into particular time slots. You must enter the location within the time range specified on your ticket. Once inside, you are welcome to stay and explore for as long as you want throughout the site's regular hours.

3. Professional guides: It is required to be accompanied by a professional guide to enter specific places of Machu Picchu, such as the Sun Gate and the Inca Bridge. Hiring a guide is strongly advised to improve your understanding and appreciation of the historical and cultural value of the site.

4. Stay on approved paths: It is critical to stay on designated trails and avoid venturing into restricted areas in order to protect the integrity of the site and

prevent harm. Signs and barricades have been installed to orient visitors and safeguard the archaeological structures.

5. Drones and heavy camera equipment are absolutely prohibited within the Machu Picchu area. Large camera equipment, such as tripods and professional video equipment may also necessitate special licenses. It is best to verify with the authorities or your tour operator for specific photography equipment regulations.

6. Consumption of food or liquids (besides water) is not permitted within the Machu Picchu site. Meals and snacks can be consumed in specified areas outside the door.

7. Smoking and trash are strictly forbidden on the premises. It is also critical to properly dispose of rubbish and to respect the environment by not littering.

8. Respectful behavior is demanded of visitors, who are expected to respect the place, its cultural significance, and other visitors. To maintain a

tranquil atmosphere, avoid touching or climbing on the archaeological structures and be cautious of noise levels.

By following these rules, you may help to preserve Machu Picchu while also ensuring a happy and respectful experience for yourself and other visitors.

What are the lodging choices around Machu Picchu

There are multiple lodging options near Machu Picchu to accommodate all budgets and interests. Here are several possibilities:

1. Aguas Calientes (Machu Picchu Pueblo): This is the most convenient spot to stay and is located at the base of Machu Picchu. There are a variety of hotels, hostels, lodges, and guesthouses with varying amenities and price points. Aguas Calientes is close to the Machu Picchu site and has restaurants, stores, and other amenities.

Luxury lodges: There are luxury lodges in the nearby locations for those looking for a more upmarket and immersive experience. These lodges frequently offer exquisite lodgings, first-rate service, and breathtaking views of the surrounding mountains and valleys.

2. Accommodations in the Sacred Valley: If you prefer to remain in a more serene setting while seeing other surrounding attractions, you can stay in the Sacred Valley. Throughout the valley, there are several hotels and resorts that provide a tranquil and scenic environment. You can easily reach Ollantaytambo, Pisac, Maras, and other Incan remains from the Sacred Valley.

3. Camping: If you're going on a multi-day journey, such as the Inca Trail or other treks, camping is frequently included in the trekking package. The trip companies offer tents and camping equipment, and camping areas are designated and maintained along the walk routes.

Consider aspects such as location, facilities, reviews, and price while selecting hotels. It's best to reserve your accommodations ahead of time, especially during high season, to ensure you get your chosen selections. There are possibilities to enhance your experience near Machu Picchu, whether you're seeking for budget-friendly solutions or opulent retreats.

CHAPTER TEN

Conclusion

Finally, Machu Picchu is a location that captures the hearts of visitors from all over the world. This ancient Incan city high in the Andes provides a really one-of-a-kind and awe-inspiring experience. Machu Picchu is a destination that makes an unforgettable imprint on those who visit, from its rich history and cultural significance to its spectacular natural beauty.

A trip to Machu Picchu necessitates meticulous planning and preparation. There are numerous factors to consider, ranging from getting permissions and selecting the best time to travel to arranging transportation and accommodations. However, the work is definitely worth it because the payoff is an unbelievable once-in-a-lifetime adventure.

The trip to Machu Picchu is loaded with breathtaking scenery and historic sites, whether you travel the Inca Trail, explore alternate trekking routes, or take the train. Aside from the primary attraction, there are various more sites to see in the Sacred Valley, including Pisac, Moray, and Maras, which provide additional insight into the Incan civilisation.

Immersion in local culture, traditional cuisine, and acclimatization to high altitude are all part of the Machu Picchu experience. Responsible tourist practices, such as respecting the property and its restrictions and being environmentally conscious, are critical to preserving this great location for future generations.

Machu Picchu entices adventurers, history buffs, and environment enthusiasts alike. It invites you to travel back in time, admire old architecture, and experience the breathtaking beauty of the Andean scenery. So, embark on this incredible voyage and watch the mysticism of Machu Picchu emerge before your eyes. It is a site that will leave you speechless, eternally carved in your mind as a tribute to human creativity and the world's wonders.

Recommendations

Machu Picchu is a place that promises a once-in-a-lifetime experience. Keep the following tips in mind as you plan your trip to this historic wonder:

1. Plan ahead of time: Because Machu Picchu is a famous tourist site, you should plan and schedule your trip well in advance. This includes obtaining permissions, arranging transportation, and making hotel reservations.

2. When deciding on the best time to come, keep the weather, crowd levels, and your particular tastes in mind. The dry season has clearer skies, whilst the wet season has lush landscapes. Shoulder seasons might offer a fair balance of beautiful weather and fewer tourists.

3. Prepare for altitude: Machu Picchu is located at a high height, thus appropriate acclimatization is essential. Before visiting Machu Picchu, spend a few days in Cusco or other high-altitude regions. Stay hydrated, avoid strenuous activity for the time being, and pay attention to your body.

4. Respect the place and local culture: Machu Picchu is a UNESCO World Heritage site that must be treated with care. Follow the rules, stay on the authorized walkways, and avoid touching or climbing on the structures. Respect local culture, interact with residents with courtesy, and encourage environmentally friendly tourism activities.

5. Pack essentials like comfortable walking shoes, layers of clothing for changing weather, a hat, sunscreen, bug repellant, and a reusable water bottle. Remember to bring your camera to capture the stunning moments.

6. Hiring a guide can enhance your trip by providing historical and cultural insights. They can help you traverse the site and understand its value.

7. Immerse yourself in local food: Try traditional Peruvian dishes and learn about the local cuisine. Don't pass up the chance to eat ceviche, quinoa-based cuisine, and Peruvian delicacies such as lomo saltado and pachamanca.

Remember that Machu Picchu is a voyage of discovery, history, and natural beauty, not just a destination. Take the time to immerse yourself in its enchantment, visit the surrounding locations, and really enjoy the experience. Allow yourself to be awestruck by the amazing architecture, breathtaking panoramas, and rich cultural legacy that surrounds this incredible location. Machu Picchu awaits, eager to leave an indelible mark on your heart and spirit.

Memories for a Lifetime

Visiting Machu Picchu is a once-in-a-lifetime opportunity that will leave you with ever lasting memories. You'll be taken to a world of wonder and discovery the moment you step foot on the ancient Incan grounds. The stunning scenery, impressive ruins, and rich history will captivate your senses and leave an everlasting imprint on your heart.

The architectural brilliance and precise details that have endured the passage of time will astound you as you tour the main sites and structures of Machu

Picchu. As you take in the panoramic views from various vantage points, the Sun Gate (Inti Punku), Huayna Picchu, and Machu Picchu Mountain will present you with awe-inspiring vistas and a sense of accomplishment.

The Inca Trail or other trekking paths will take you through a variety of scenery, from steep mountains to lush woods, and will reward you with a sense of adventure and personal triumph. Each step along the old routes will bring you closer to the mythical city, gradually revealing its secrets.

The nearby sights, including as the Sacred Valley, Pisac, Moray, and Maras, will give you a better knowledge of the Incan culture and its relationship with nature. You'll see their agricultural terraces' creativity, the accuracy of their stonework, and the spiritual importance imbued in every structure.

Your contacts with the local culture and cuisine will enrich your recollections even more. Interacting with the friendly and hospitable Peruvians, learning about their traditions, and experiencing the tastes of their classic cuisine will leave an indelible mark on your taste buds and your heart.

But, beyond the concrete sights and flavors, memories that elicit a sense of surprise, astonishment, and personal growth are the ones that will last. The peaceful contemplation amidst the old remains, the sense of connection to the past, and the appreciation for being allowed to witness such a beautiful location will stay with you for the rest of your life.

So, when you set off on your adventure to Machu Picchu, enjoy every minute, immerse yourself in the enchantment of the surrounds, and let the awe of this wonderful place permeate into your spirit. Allow the memories you make to become treasured keepsakes, reminding you of the ancient wonder's tremendous beauty and significance. Machu Picchu will always have a special place in your heart as a reminder of humanity's amazing achievements and the continuing spirit of exploration.

Printed in Great Britain
by Amazon

31972308R10096

ICON OF GENTLENESS

SAINT NICHOLAS

J M Rosenthal

Revised 2020

Paperback: 978-1-949570-95-3
Ebook: 978-1-949570-96-0

LCCN: 2020925223

St Nicholas belongs to everyone.

Though most know him now as Santa Claus or Father Christmas, his true identity and his legends and miracles reflect the desire of a man who, as a bishop of the church, sought to share his faith with those he came in contact with day by day through many extraordinary acts of kindness.

His message of care and the need to support one's neighbour echoes from the 4th century when he lived and worked in Asia Minor in what is now known as Turkey. His message of gentleness, strength of belief and his unwavering compassion is needed as much today as it was then. In this spirit we begin our search for St Nicholas, Wonderworker and our Friend in Heaven.

Long live St Nicholas!

Each year we celebrate with joy the coming
Of that great Saint of old, we love so dear.
His legends are the stories we all cherish,
They call to mind that Christmas now is near!

O great St Nicholas, we hail and greet you,
We thank you for the good news that you bring.
O lead us on to Bethlehem, the Manger,
Where we can pray and joyous songs forever sing.

Your love of children, marks your way of caring.
The students three, new life you bring to be.
The sailors, soldiers and the ones in prison,
Your power and prayer, the miracles we see.

Dear saint, your name brings hope and consolation
To people poor and those who suffer wrong.
The celebrations and the joy and splendour
Become the theme and message of our song.

We now receive the gifts you freely give us,
As tokens of your generosity,
That we must imitate and share the goodness
We at this season in each other see.

TEXT: J M Rosenthal, 2010
TUNE: Londonderry Air

The truth of your dealings, our Father and Bishop Nicholas,
showed you to your flock as a standard of faith, as the icon of
gentleness, and as a teacher of self-discipline. By lowliness you
attained to the heights, by poverty to great riches.

…English translation from the Orthodox
Liturgy for St Nicholas Day

Now the story begins.

Nicholas was born in 260 AD into a very wealthy family and raised in Patara, a seaside Lycian beauty spot still known to tourists and locals alike on the Mediterranean coast. Patara's seaport, complete with its striking blue water, and it incredible monuments, stone structures and its once grand amphitheatre, all contribute to its overall splendour.

Nicholas' parents, Ona and Theopannes found that even at a very early age that Nicholas was a unique child. Legend has it that when he was placed in the bath he stood up strong and tall with hands folded as in prayer as he was bathed. It was said that Nicholas also refrained from nourishment from his mother's breast on Wednesdays and Fridays, thus honoring the Christian virtue of fasting on these traditional days of abstinence, yes even from his infancy.

As he grew, Nicholas became the epitome of the meaning of his name, "victor of the people". He led a privileged life and early years were full of joy.

However, soon that would change. A plague struck in Patara and many of the citizens became ill and died. Nicholas' parents were to be victims of that plague. This great loss came when Nicholas was still very young. He did, however, inherit the great wealth of his family, administered by his uncle, a priest. Nicholas always remem-bered how his parents lived according to the highest Christian principles. He soon was placed in the care of that uncle, the Abbot of a monastic-like community in Lycia, where again, Christian values of unconditional love and inclusion of all, were part of his maturing process.

The early days of Nicholas new life were shocking to him and challenged his faith. Many poor and outcast persons made their way to the church door day by day. This experience helped him recognize and respond to needs and the gross injustice that now confronted him in his daily life. The people who flocked to the church for all kinds of help would not only influence Nicholas' future, but would produce the saint beloved the world over to this very day.

It was apparent as he grew older, although very popular now with his uncle's community, he would not want to carry out his life confined to the cell of a monastic-style living. It was recognised that Nicholas had the vocation of a priest and that his desire was to be with the local common people. He would become a beloved parish priest.

It is in this role Nicholas became even more strikingly aware of the plight of those about him, especially the poor. The local village was a refuge for many in need. This awareness and his instinctive love for people led the young priest to be generous in giving money and other types of help to those in trouble. And help them he did. The legends abound. Of course, because of this generosity, his fame spread throughout the land even though he always asked the recipients of his largess to give thanks God, never him!

Nicholas had a special love for children. He remembered vividly the wonderful childhood he had and how good his parents were to him and all they taught him. It is no wonder that in history his being patron saint of children would be his best-known title. Nicholas went about doing good, constantly.

One afternoon during adoration prayers in the village chapel Nicholas fell asleep. In his dream he had a vision of Jesus Christ handing him the book of the Gospels and St Mary placing a pallium (a symbol of the bishop) over his shoulders. Jesus told him he must work among the people if he wanted to receive the crown of life. He had no clue what it might actually mean.

A startled Nicholas awoke from his sleep riddled with deep concern over his dream and what he might mean for him. He didn't seem to understand, yet in just a few months he would come to grasp what God had in mind for his life.

As a young priest Father Nicholas saw his duty to God and God's people as his only vocation. He took his vows seriously and he made it a habit to visit the cathedral in Myra every morning, very early, to say his own prayers before the rigours of his day began.

Later that year the old bishop of Myra died. The church leaders assembled in Myra to select someone to take his place. The council met for several days and had great difficulty coming to a decision on who was to be the bishop of this important diocese, a part of the world struggling with pagan customs and with hints of persecution abounding.

Finally an elderly official told the assembly of a dream he had had the night before, one that would change Christian history. In the dream the Lord spoke to the man and said, "Tomorrow morning the first person to enter the cathedral is to be the next bishop - his name will be Nicholas". The council prayed for guidance. Could the dream provide the answer to their dilemma? Who was this Nicholas of the dream?

As the bells of the angelus rang in the cathedral tower at 6 a.m. and the great doors were opened by the verger, young Nicholas made his way to the altar rail to pray as was his normal custom in visiting the cathedral every day.

As he entered he was immediately stopped by the elderly church leader who had shared his dream with his fellow leaders. "Young man," he said, "tell me your name." Nicholas responded dutifully, "Sir, my name is Nicholas, your servant for Jesus Christ's sake." The old man embraced him and signaled the rest of the assembly to join him. The dream was true. A bewildered Nicholas did not know what was happening. The old man escorted the startled Nicholas to the bishop's throne and exclaimed, "You are to be our bishop!" Nicholas gasped with shock and said this could not be, "I am only a young priest". "Long live Bishop Nicholas," the assembly sang and the cathedral was filled with alleluias and shouts of thanks to God.

He then remembered his own dream. Nicholas knelt down and prayed. This was no dream now!

News of Nicholas' selection as the next bishop spread rapidly through the diocese. The people were very happy indeed. In just weeks Nicholas was brought to the cathedral from his church, along with his uncle and all the clergy from where he had lived, and a great procession made its way through the streets. Thousands cheered as Nicholas entered the cathedral, to reappear soon as Nicholas, Bishop of Myra. He wore the great bishop's gold mitre and splendid cloth of gold cope. He carried the shiny crozier, the sign of being a shepherd to his people complete with staff!

Seemingly hours later, the crowds of those unable to enter the church, saw the great doors open. Into their midst came Bishop Nicholas. He blessed them and the diocese and city. Singing and cheering filled the air.

As foretold in the dream, he now wore the pallium and held the gospel book It all began to make sense to him.

The love of the people of Myra for their bishop grew stronger day by day. Myra was a unique city. Its name meant "the most brilliant". St Paul visited Myra as recorded in the Bible in the book of Acts. He met here with his followers on their way to Rome.

By the second century Myra was the centre of Christian activities in this region complete with its Lycian rock tombs. Nicholas became bishop in the 4th century. This did not mean the church had a comfortable existence.

Pagan deities still reigned in some people's hearts and minds. Threats to Christians were common place.

Nicholas's episcopate was to be an eventful one. His compassion and care, for which he was renowned, would not cease in his new office but ever increase. He used the power and strength of his office to seek justice for all and to influence those who could help make life better for the people in his care.

One of greatest stories of the beloved saint is that of the man who had three daughters who were of the age to be married. Custom would dictate that the father of the women, in this case a rather poor man, needed to provide a dowry for each of his daughters in order that they could be married. It was an impossible task. The women were desperate. The father at wits end.

Thus the father, not knowing what to do for himself or his daughters, decided that he would sell the daughters one by one, into the slavery or prostitution. This became a community scandal and a situation that reached the ears of young Nicholas.

Realizing that his financial wealth could assist this desperate scenario Nicholas began to think of ways he could anonymously get gold coins into the hands of the father so the daughters would escape such a gruesome fate.

Nicholas had a plan. Approaching the home of the father and three daughters he climbed up on the roof and placed a bag of

gold into the chimney. Legend says the gold landed in stockings that were hanging near the fire to dry.

In the morning the father found the gold and was overcome with happiness as now at least one daughter could be saved. Money enough for one dowry. In the midst of all the excitement the father wondered where the money came from and was quite perplexed. Although the family rejoiced that now the oldest daughter could be saved, the other two faced the perils of disgrace.

The next night Nicholas repeated the surprise visit and delivered the second bag of gold. The father, still wondering how this could be happening, could now offer his second daughter a better life.

The father, fully realising and praying that a third bag of gold might be forthcoming decided that he would stay up all night to see who this agent of goodwill might be. Nicholas carefully approached the house during the night and climbed onto the roof and delivered the bag of gold as usual. As the gold hit the stocking the father opened the window and called to the shadowy figure moving away. Getting no response, he opened the door and chased the gift-bearer down the city streets. Catching up to the cloaked stranger he grabbed at his robe and turning the man around saw that is was Nicholas.

The father fell on his knees praising and thanking Nicholas for his generosity. Nicholas quickly rebuked the man and told him to rise and to thank God alone for providing these gifts.

This loving act lifted the burden of need for a very grateful father. It also paved the way for each of the three young women to live their own lives fully in the world. Nicholas' example and its effect can be seen in the Christmas offerings that bring joy to people to this day. The legend of the three daughters is likely where the idea of holiday presents and especially the Christmas stocking all began. It teaches the joy of giving as well as the gift of receiving from others. It is these events that would create the image of St Nicholas as gift-giver, and indeed the true name of the one now called Santa Claus or Father Christmas.

In another legend, the governor had taken a bribe to condemn three innocent men. At the time set for their execution Bishop Nicholas appeared at the site and stayed the hands of the executioners, releasing the prisoners. He then turned to the governor and would not relent until the official admitted his crime and expressed his penitence in the full hearing of the people.

Another legend tells of the imprisonment of three imperial officers who were on their way to Phyrgia. Later when they were back in Constantinople the jealousy of the prefect Ablavius caused them to be imprisoned on false charges and an order for their death was procured from the emperor. Realising their fate, the desperate officers remembered hearing how Bishop Nicholas had interceded for other falsely accused persons, they prayed to God that through Christ's merits and Nicholas' intercession they might be saved.

Nicholas appeared to them and blessed them. That same night Nicholas appeared to the emperor in a dream and told him, with a severe warning, to release the three innocent men. Ablavius the prefect experienced the same exact dream. In the morning the emperor and the prefect compared notes and spoke of each other's dreams. The falsely accused men were sent for and questioned.

When the officials heard that the prisoners had called on the name of Nicholas, remembering the terror of their dreams, the men were instantly freed.

Another legend deals with the fact that Nicholas was very strong in his faith. Indeed, being a man of firm convictions, Nicholas' anger mounted when he, by chance, came across a temple of a pagan goddess in the forest outside Myra. Seeing people he knew at the shrine, he compelled them to leave, and in an act of defiance against the pagan god, he destroyed the image and sealed off the temple.

But the pagan deities plotted against the saint and his church. One story tells of an elderly women asking some merchant sailors to deliver a container of special fragrant oil to the bishop's church in Myra and to anoint the walls with it, as a gift from the grateful woman. As the vessel set sail, Nicholas appeared to the captain and warned him of a great danger that had come his way. "Where is the oil the elderly woman (really a witch!) gave you to deliver to Myra?" he said.

Handing the oil to Nicholas, the saint threw the substance into the sea. Flames shot up all around the boat. Had the oil been delivered and used, the church would have been destroyed.

Calming the sea seemingly was one of Nicholas' most often recalled miracles and on his voyage from visiting the Holy Land, where to this day there is the St Nicholas Cave in Beit Jala, the stormy sea whispers peace at the intercession of this man of God.

In another story, the brave Nicholas, during a great famine, convinces a ship's captain that some of the grain on his ship must be left in Myra to feed the hungry. The ship, coming from the east, had a large storage of grain heading for Cairo. If he were to give any of the wheat to Nicholas, those awaiting the shipment would punish him for stealing. Not being able to say no to our saint, the captain unloads some grain and the people were saved. Upon arrival at his final destination, the captain, now a man of great faith finds the store of the grain, full, nothing missing! He has now learned the reward of helping others in distress.

There is the story of young Adeodatus, who being abducted by the Saracens as a slave, is returned miraculously by the saint to his parents after they pray for their son. Thus St Nicholas becomes protector of the human family.

The most memorable miracle concerns the mystical number three again. This time it is three children kidnapped by a rural butcher and innkeeper, murdered and put into brine for pickling. There was a famine and food was scarce. Bishop Nicholas' arrival in the country inn was truly miraculous. The bishop was offered meat for his supper. Nicholas thought, how could this be, in the midst of the famine! He prayed. Suddenly he arose and went into the kitchen. The butcher was standing at the barrel. Exposing the murderous act of the butcher, he thrust his hand into the brine barrel, the three boys were at once restored, and began praising Nicholas. At once, the bishop halted their words and told them to praise God alone for this wondrous act.

All his wondrous favours and acts of kindness continue to be known to people of goodwill in all times and places.

Persecution for Christians arose in the land. When Nicholas would face imprisonment it would not be in the company of murders and thieves and robbers but with fellow bishops, priests and deacons. There was no room in the prisons at the time of Christian persecution for those who actually were condemned of notorious crimes. The persecution ended with the arrival of Constantine. Thus a new age began with Christians free to worship, as they desired. Free at last, Nicholas continues steadfast in his episcopal duties. Yet the church still was facing some difficult times.

The great council of Nicaea, with bishops from all parts of the Christian Church attending, was held in 325AD. Nicholas' presence at Nicaea became one of confrontation and criticism for the normally even-tempered man. It was here that he would face Bishop Arias, a name now associated with one of the great heresies and early false teachings concerning Jesus Christ. As Arias spoke Nicholas' fury welled up and he eventually confronted the man and legend says he slapped him in the face. Nicholas was reprimanded by his fellow bishops, who although they agreed with him, felt his actions were unfortunate. Nicholas was suspended from his duties for a time but soon all was forgiven and his preaching and teaching flourished until his death.

The Christian faith formulated at Nicaea is still confessed in most Roman Catholic, Anglican, Orthodox, and Lutheran churches in the words of what is called the Nicene Creed.

The trumpet call sounded and the echo of "servant well-done" heralded the news that Nicholas had died. It was December 6th in 343AD.

To this very day his now empty tomb and the foundations of the original Church dedicated to him are still found in the city that is now also named Demre and Myra.

The glories of Myra came to a halt for the Christian community when the town and church were destroyed during saracen raids in 7th and 9th centuries and then yet again severe destruction took place in 1034.

However in 1087 merchant sailors from Bari Italy arrived in what was left of Myra and forcefully removed the bones (relics) of the beloved saint that were buried in the church and, rather appropriately by sea, took them to Southern Italy. The Myra church that remains, although incomplete in its structure, was built in the 9th century and restored several times including a major restoration in the 20th century.

This work was done by Greek archaeologists who reconstructed the centuries old ruined church in 1964. With the help of the Russian Orthodox Church, as Russians flock to both Bari and Myra/Demre, other improvements continue to be made One can still see the original floor mosaics and frescos on the wall.

As one of the most popular saints, many attempts were made to honour his memory. Nicholas' importance was recognised by the

Emperor Justinian, who had a magnificent church built to honour
the Saint in Constantinople.

Sing we now and chant it
For St Nicholas is here—
December now brings us
The day we love so dear.

He comes with gifts and stories true—
He tells us what we ought to do.
The world's a better place to be
When now, our saint we can see.
His wonders and his legends told,
The stories, miracles, so bold
Love's message that his presence sends—
The sailors, children's friend.
Three girls are saved, the grain increased,
The innocent they now go free,
The three small boys come back to life,
He calms the deep blue sea.
From Myra came he so long ago,
The myrrh his wonders still do show.
The Bari pilgrims make their way
For at his shrine they pray.
With Nicholas we all await
The coming of the Saviour great.
Our saint, he humbly bends the knee,
As Christ the Lord we see.

Text: J M Rosenthal, 2007
Tune: O, kom er eens kijken
(Dutch Sinterklaas tune)

ST NICHOLAS TODAY

To this very day in Germany, Austria, Luxembourg, Czech Republic, Poland, Switzerland, Netherlands and Belgium men still dress in bishop's garb to be St Nicholas, making various appearances from late November until December 5 and 6.

These "saints" quiz children on their prayers, school work, and church attendance, urge them to be good and give them gifts. Some children still leave straw and carrots for St Nicholas' horse and place them in front of the fireplace. What they expect in the morning is that the straw and carrots become presents, sweets and toys. In some parts of the world St Nicholas collects children lists, naming the gifts they wish to receive from the Christ Child (Christkind) at Christmas or the Three Kings at Epiphany (January 6). One does need to note the tradition, as it is often seen, in Austria is less than desirable. The image of Krampus, a devil figure, often overshadows (unofficially) the good saint. Germany, too, uses the name Nikolaus but often the image is a good ole Santa.

(The use of the name Nicholas is a good start to re-introduce the true identity of our saint, but any "helpers" need to be carefully selected and their purpose thought through fully.)

Pictures of Nicholas often show three bags of gold next to him and often these bags become three discs or balls, the symbol of the pawn broker's industry. The number 3 plays an important part in the stories of Nicholas as we have seen with the saving of the three women and the three pickled boys.

In some countries, people receive gifts on St Nicholas Day. In many churches, institutions and homes the custom of wrapping a present on St Nicholas eve for someone in need or for a homeless shelter or home for children has become the tradition. In some churches, the entire congregation bring gifts for the poor that are distributed during the Advent season.

Nicholas' name appears, with Christianity's major saints, in the Orthodox liturgy of St John

Chrysostom and his life as a bishop is seen as a model for other bishops by that church. His day is marked on most church calendars on December 6 or in some Orthodox traditions December 19.

Many places honour him as their patron or at the very least, a special saint: Greece, Russia, the kingdom of Naples, Sicily, Lorraine, Liege and any cities in Italy, Germany, Austria, Belgium, Campen in the Netherlands, Corfu in Greece, Fribourg in Switzerland and Moscow in Russia. He is a patron of mariners, merchants, bankers, travellers, and children.

There are towns and villages named for the saint in Wales, Austria,

Belgium, England, Cuba, Argentina, Venezuela, and France. Although veneration of St Nicolai is prominent in Russia he is not their patron saint.

Alas, it is St Andrew. Nicholas is represented in art, in association with his legendary miracles and as a Santa Claus/Father Christmas image.

Each year in May, to mark the celebration of the arrival or translation of the relics (bones) of the saint to Italy, the city of Bari has a great festival from 7-10 May. Bari is the main Nicholas Shrine for the Christian World, and people flock there in the thousands. Still to this day, and as a sign of authenticity, the relics release a liquid substance, called manna, complete with a sweet myrrh fragrance, that has been associated with healing, prayer and pilgrimage for many years.

The Dominican Order serves the shrine and its ecumenical work. The Prior withdraws the manna each May 9 during a Solemn Mass and procession to the crypt tomb in the basilica. The celebration includes taking a bigger than life size statue of the Saint in Bari on the sea and then re-enacting the actual arrival accompanied by fireworks, even in daylight.

A pageant "storico" parade makes it way through the old city, with live representations of the historic tale of the coming of St Nicholas to the port city. Officials in Turkey, seemingly aware of the importance of the relics of the saint for tourism, have made attempts to have the relics returned.

The people of Bari simply say, "it will never happen!"

Although Christian worship is longer normative in the area of Myra, or better put "not tolerated" in Turkey, the local businesses do well with selling some rather nice souvenirs and religious icons made of wax. Authorities need a push from other countries to change their attitude toward religion. Removal of a religious statue, donated by Moscow officials, from the town centre in Demre was a most unfortunate move.

Other places have relics of the saint, most significantly in St Nicolas de Port, Lorraine, France, Flushing, New York, Beit Jala, Palestine. In Lorraine a procession of a statue and relics is held on Whitmonday, with incense blazing and joyous singing of French Nicolas carols. Candlelit processions mark the December 6 feast in this sleepy industrial village, a place adorned with a massive

church named for the saint. There is a unique art form in nearby Epinal that is very popular.

December 5 and 6, and indeed as early as mid-November, communities celebrate St Nicholas' arrival for the season and the actual holy day itself. Holland, Belgium, France and even Canterbury England now have annual events. Each June an Italian Puglia group in Chicago sponsor a San Nicola di Bari celebration as well, including the visit of their statue to the great Lake Michigan, modelled after the custom in Bari of taking the saint on a boat, marking his "arrival" in Italy in 1087 AD.

St Nicholas Day, in the dark of night, in Kussnacht am Rigi Switzerland, is the setting for a unique celebration. Hundreds of men of the St Nicholas Society parade through the streets of the idyllic village wearing large candle-lit bishop's miters, called ifellen, accompanied by cracking whips, Swiss horns and cow bells and the Saint himself with his "black" men. A true example of "light shining in the darkness". It was the invention of Franz Sidler some 75 years ago.

In a Lutheran congregation in Detroit, Michigan, one can have brunch, the great American meal, with St Nicholas and in the one-time Dutch populated cities of Holland, Michigan, Pella, Iowa and others, Sinterklaas, the Dutch name for Sint Nicolaas, still makes his appearance to the delight of the children and museums and art galleries display Nicholas artefacts. Many embassies and consulates of countries where St Nicholas Day is observed have a celebration, usually inviting a wide range of guests. St Nicholas is known in Africa in the bishop's guise, a window of St Mary's Cathedral Johannesburg attests to that and a Dutch priest in Sudan thrills young people as he dons the colourful apparel of Bishop Nicholas.

There are also the Medieval Mystery Plays of St Nicholas, such as that of Jean Bodel of Arras, France, and many carols and hymns like this one sung at Great Hormead in England:

No Bishop ere was more beloved
By young and old than he.
Wherever Santa Claus is known
His name shall honoured be!

Churches of all denominations hold services in December to honour Nicolas, Bishop and Saint, and new groups of enthusiasts are working for the restoration of the Nicholas customs are being organised in the USA and the United Kingdom. Among them are the St Nicholas Center in Holland, Michigan USA and the St Nicholas Society in England, a sister organisation to the Saint Nicolaas Genootschap in Flanders and in the Netherlands.

In the Norfolk town of North Walsham, England, the parish celebrates the feast with great ceremony including appointing a boy bishop.

This hymn is also sung in the Norfolk village:

Saint Nicholas the Shepherd true
Who brought his flock to faith anew
Now by his prayers and faith secure
Draws us, in Jesus, to endure.

THAL

The Boy Bishop ceremony is still held at Hereford Cathedral each year and a tomb of a Boy Bishop rests in the nave floor of Salisbury Cathedral. The custom speaks to the young age at which Nicholas was consecrated as a Bishop. Other English parishes observe the day of the saint with unique activities. St Nicholas, New Romney, Kent has a boy bishop light the Advent wreath candles each week. In many churches, attention is drawn to collecting toys, goods, money and food for the needy, as Nicholas would want us to do, as at Marston Parish Church in the Oxford Diocese. St Nicholas, Karoo has 'Operation St Nicholas' with a complete programme of helping the poor, including refugee camps and orphanages in Eastern Europe. Santa St Nick visits St Nicholas Church, Strood, Kent after a Toy Service where gifts are collected for children in need. This is also celebrated at St James Merton and St Nicholas at Wade UK.

Likely the most famous church dedicated to St Nicholas is King's College Chapel, Cambridge, with the co-patronage of Our Lady. The Anglican Cathedral in Seoul, Korea also has this dual dedication, as does the main parish church in Liverpool, Lancing College, and Wilton, England. The most dramatic music that honours Nicholas is the Cantata written for Lancing College by Benjamin Britten with the text by Eric Crozier. Some churches use the St Nicholas Mass by Haydn at Christmas Midnight Mass. St Nicholas is the patron saint of the beloved Royal School of Church Music.

Nearly 400 churches bear the Nicholas name in the UK, including the cathedral in Newcastle Upon Tyne. In the Orthodox world hundreds of churches are named for him and almost every church anywhere has an icon of the saint in full view. The St Nicholas Russian Cathedral in Washington DC is wall to wall with murals of the saint's life. The Orthodox Cathedral in Tokyo Japan is called "Nikolai-Do" - Nicholas' house, also honouring the great missionary St Nicholas of Japan, whose life was influenced by St Nicholas. St Luke's Episcopal Church has an impressive shrine in their Germantown Philadelphia Church.

In Florida a Baptist Church is found called St Nicholas and in Scotland a number of Presbyterian Churches are dedicated to St Nicholas, including a grand Kirk in Aberdeen, where the main shopping mall is also St Nicholas. Another large shopping mall is St Nicholas Centre near Wimbledon in Sutton. At one-time St Nicholas Reformed Church, cathedral-like in stature, stood at 48th and 5th Avenue, New York. Its loss is tragic as is, of course, is that New York is also home to the Greek Orthodox Church of our saint destroyed on September 11, 2001 during the terrorist attack on the World Trade Center. The long-awaited construction of the new church is finally happening and will be a lasting memorial to all that reminds the world of 9/11

Landmark St John the Divine Episcopal Cathedral has the saint above the baptistry door, with St Nicholas Avenue, just nearby. On this street one finds St Nick's Pub, St Nicholas Optical Shop and almost anything imaginable named for our Nick. A marvellous authentic Bari-styled restaurant exists in Paoli, Pennsylvania, complete with its name San Nicola and a St Nicholas charity tree during Advent. We long for the release of Gerald Hartke's full length film, Nicholas of Myra, filmed entirely in the state of New York. St James Episcopal Cathedral was first to host an extensive St Nicholas Center (www.stnicholascenter.org) exhibition.

Churches often have stained glass windows or images even if the church is not named for the saint. Some of the most outstanding in the UK are: All Saints, Hillesden; St Sepulchre, London; Croydon Minster; St Thomas, Salisbury; Salisbury Cathedral (5 images); St John the Baptist,

Newcastle; St Matthew's Westminster; Chichester Cathedral Cloister; Winchester Cathedral (French font); and Holy Trinity, Stratford Upon Avon. St Nicholas Chapels are found in Canterbury Cathedral; St Dunstan's Canterbury; Christ the King Roman Catholic Cathedral, Liverpool, and York Minster.

A major permanent exhibition of St Nicholas is found at the Episcopal Church's Virginia Theological Seminary in Alexandria USA. The vast display includes teaching aids and resources for churches, schools and home use. This is the gift of Carol P Myers who also operates the on-line

St Nicholas Centre.

Three English pubs are named for St Nick: Stevenage, Carlisle and Bristol. The demoting of St Nicholas by the Roman Catholic Church to an optional "memorial" has actually triggered a new spark of interest in him it seems, at least in religious circles. The Protestant refusal to welcome the saint-tradition in severe parts of Holland might also be a factor as to why the Damrak in Amsterdam, not known for its religious fervour, sees greater and greater numbers as children and parents flock to great Sint Nicolaas as he arrives each November. He comes from Spain by boat, mounts his white horse, complete with dozens of Piet (Pete) helpers, and offers sweets and candy to the children, riding through the vast city for several hours. Commonly called Sinterklaas - this is the sad source of the name Santa Claus, as the Dutch reached New Amsterdam with their traditions. Each year there is an exhibition in the Chapel of the Lord in the Attic on the canal behind St Nicholas Church in Amsterdam.

The Dutch arrival comes about the third weekend in November; in order for the saint to makes his rounds and check on the good and bad children, thus determining the end results for December 5. Shop keepers and businesses benefit from the early arrival as well. In many parts of Holland gifts are given only on St Nicholas Day, not at Christmas, which is viewed only in a purely religious observance. There are St Nicholas special sweets and decorations everywhere.

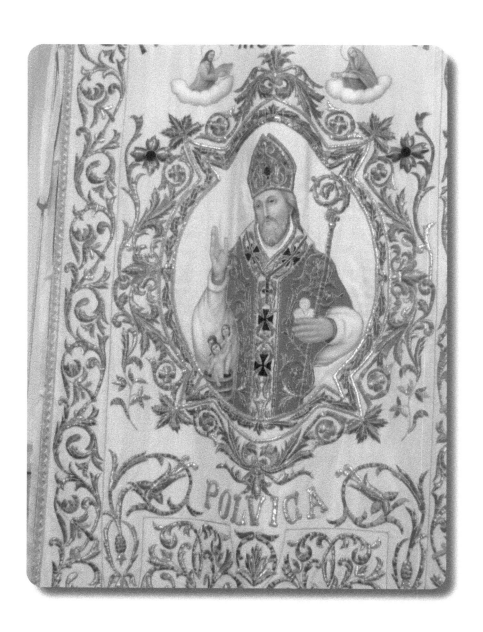

OUR FRIEND IN HEAVEN……

Legends captivate the mind and heart of the reader as they allow people to escape to the realm where one can only wish such experiences are completely and fully real.

Saint Nicholas, the Christian gift to young and old alike, is associated with stories and legends that have been woven into the celebration of Christmas. In addition to the story of the birth of Jesus Christ and the events in Holy Bethlehem, St Nicholas, also now known to the world as Father Christmas or Santa Claus, can be a means of securing a spiritual dimension to this festive time of the year. For indeed St Nicholas, lover of the poor and patron saint of children, is a primary example of how Christians are meant to live their lives on this earthly pilgrimage.

A priest, a bishop, Nicholas put Jesus Christ at the centre of his life, his ministry and his entire existence. He is our friend in heaven and there is a bit of him in all of us I am sure.

The apparent transformation of St Nicholas into a more secular symbol needs to be addressed boldly with an enthusiasm for the customs and traditions surrounding St Nicholas and an implementation of such traditions in our churches, schools and communities. We ignore St Nicholas to our peril. Santa Claus, as he is most popularly known, deserves to have his true identity named so all can hear his story. The name St Nicholas, of course, often lingers in the background, especially in Europe. Even in the USA.

The most beloved fiction story of Christmastide is THE VISIT FROM ST NICHOLAS-Clement

Moore the said author, himself an Anglican, has the name St Nicholas clearly as the title of the much longed for visitor.

'Twas the night before Christmas, when all through the house
Not a creature was stirring, not even a mouse;
The stockings were hung by the chimney with care,
In hopes that St. Nicholas soon would be there;

New York can still claim St Nicholas as their very own, if indeed they were so inclined! New Amsterdam certainly knew St Nicholas well. The New York of the English would be the turning point, and a loss of a great tradition.

One of the longest streets in New York is St Nicholas Avenue.

Some say as time evolves that there will be many a young child that will not know the truth about Christmas and its sacred origin.

Restoring the tradition also means parents never have to lie to their children again. Nicholas was a real person, not an flying elf!

Santa, by his very nature, often distracts or even becomes a substitute for the Holy Child of Mary and Joseph. For such persons, and indeed by its own merit, St Nicholas in his proper role, can help lead us beyond ourselves and beyond him, as an icon of gentleness, to the manger "to see this thing that has come to pass".

PRAYERS

Let your continual mercy O Lord enkindle in your church the never failing gift of charity, that, following the example of your servant Nicholas of Myra and aided by his prayers we may have grace to deal in generosity and love with children and all who are poor and distressed, and to uphold the cause of those who have no help; for the sake of him who gave his life for us, your son our Saviour Jesus Christ, who lives and reigns with you and the Holy Spirit, one God now and for ever. Amen

Almighty God, in your love you gave to your servant Nicholas of Myra perpetual name for deeds of kindness on land and sea; grant, we pray, that your church may never cease to work for the happiness of children, the safety of sailors, the relief of the poor and help for those tossed by the tempest of doubt or grief. Through Jesus Christ Our Lord. Amen

Nicholas, Icon of gentleness and generosity,
Nicholas, Model of meekness and charity,
Nicholas, Defender of the Christian Faith,
Nicholas, Myrrh of the fragrance of Christ,
Nicholas, Help of those who suffer wrong,
Nicholas, steward of the mysteries of God,
Nicholas, Guide of the penitent sinner,
Nicholas, Source of joy and thanksgiving,
Nicholas, Saint who points us to the Manger,
Pray for us.

Orthodox Troparion (Tone 4)

Your works of justice showed you to your congregation a canon of faith, the likeness of humility, a teacher of abstinence, O Father, Bishop Nicholas. Wherefore, by humility you achieved exaltation, and by meekness, richness. Intercede, therefore, with Christ to save our souls.

"Now bless us on the sea of life
As we against all deadly strife
Live out our lives courageously
At home, at work and on the sea
O wonderworker and our friend
Your blessings now to us extend."

Blessed Saint Nicholas, we honour you for your acts of kindness, goodwill and charity to those on the margins of life.

Inspire us with your desire for justice and joy for all people; help us learn from you what faith and action means, and make us aware of those around us.

Give us the same sense of joy you had in your ministry. And when we remember you may we also remember the Lord you loved and followed, both in times of tribulation, famine, persecution and humiliation, as well as in times of joy and peace, even Jesus Christ our Lord Amen.

Canon J M Rosenthal

Let us sing the song of Nicholas
The saint we celebrate
We are happy to remember him
His legends they are great
As he brings much happiness and joy
To every girl and boy
St Nicholas we cheer

Chorus:
Glory, glory, hallelujah
Glory, glory, hallelujah
Glory, glory, hallelujah
St Nicholas we cheer

As he saved three girls from poverty
The sailors sailed with ease
Innocent the soldiers now could be
His miracles we see
Golden balls show generosity
His bishop's robes dons he
St Nicholas we cheer

Let us be like him in all he did
For Christmas we prepare
For in Bethlehem we now can see
Jesus, his Mother's care
As we celebrate this season bright
As children of the light
St Nicholas we cheer

THE AUTHOR

Dr Jim Rosenthal, is the founder of the UK/USA Saint Nicholas Society and the authored many books and articles on 'San Nicola' and dons the robes of Bishop Nicholas to share with thousands from Canterbury to Philadelphia, the great tradition of Nicholas of Myra and Bari. He says, "There is a little bit of St Nicholas in all of us." He co-authored the book St Nicholas A Closer Look at Christmas, Nelson 2005, Nashville, USA and a devotional Advent book From Holly Jolly to Holy published by Forward Movement, USA

Saint Nicolas
Saint Nicholas
Sao Nicolau
San Nicolas
San Nicola
Sanda Necole
St Nikolai
St Nicolae
Agios Nikolaos
St Nikola
Sankt Nikolaus
Heiliger Nicolaus
Sint Niklaas
Sint Nicolaas
Sw Mikolaj
St Nicolai
Kleeschen
Mikulase

Photo by Sergio Giaccio Polvica

Nikolo
Samichlaus
Sinterklaas/Santa Claus

SPLENDID CHURCHES DEDICATED TO ST NICHOLAS

St Nicolas de Port, France (Roman Catholic)
St Nicholas Beit Jala Palestine (Orthodox)
St Nicholas at Wade, UK (Anglican)
Sint Niklaas Belgium (Roman Catholic)
San Nicolas di Bari, Madrid (Roman Catholic)
St Nicolai, Spandau, Germany (Lutheran)
St Nicholas Aberdeen (Presbyterian)
St Nicholas Chiswick, London (Anglican)
Sint Nicolaas, Amsterdam (Catholic)
St Nicholas, Prague (Protestant Hussite)
St Nicholas, Prague (Roman Catholic)
St Mary and St Nicholas Wilton (Anglican)
Our Lady and St Nicholas, Liverpool (Anglican)

The story of the great Wonderworker,
Nicholas of Myra, comes alive in this
gentle re-telling of his stories and legends.
The book is also a perfect resource for
those interested in the renewal of a great
tradition and to remind young and old
alike of the true identity of the Advent
visitor known as Santa Claus or Father
Christmas.

The real Santa Claus and Father Christ mas comes alive in this new
edition easy-to-read look at the life of this great man of generosity

and faith. This is the perfect introduction to the saint, if ignored, is to our peril as lovers of Advent and Christmas. St Nicholascards and images are found throughout the book.

THE AUTHOR

Dr James Rosenthal founded the UK Based St Nicholas Society and has authored books and articles in honour of the saint. Dr Rosenthal is an ordained Anglican priest and is originally from Chicago.

www.stnicholassociety.co.uk

St NICOLAS

Lightning Source UK Ltd.
Milton Keynes UK
UKHW021012290121
377827UK00004B/143

9 781949 570953